A Garden Can Be Anywhere

A Garden Can Be Anywhere

Creating Bountiful and Beautiful Edible Gardens

Lauri Kranz with Dean Kuipers

With photographs by Yoshihiro Makino

ABRAMS, NEW YORK

For Gus, Milo, and Spenser.
May you always have a garden in your lives.

Contents

Foreword

Seeing and feeling the plants growing there, being aware of them and where they are in their season, and cooking what's fresh changed the way we thought about our food.

It was a lucky day for me and my family seven or eight years ago when Lauri Kranz—or "Garden Lauri," as we call her—happened into our lives. Our children were at a new preschool in Los Angeles, and at the school's fund-raising auction my husband, David, and I bid on a popular item that featured this mythical character everyone was oohing and aahing over: Lauri would come to the top bidder's home to set up a kitchen garden. I will never forget the day of our first meeting when I opened our front door to find wispy and beautiful, dirt-dusted, oversize-hat-wearing Lauri at our threshold. She came in, truly like a ray of sunshine, swooping our kids up into her passion for gardening, vegetables, the land, and life itself.

As two chefs, we knew we wanted a garden, but we didn't know how much we needed it. From a patch of dry chaparral high on a hill behind our house, Lauri created a place where we would read and dream up menus while the kids played. Whenever we needed herbs or berries or some Swiss chard for dinner, it was right there, just out the kitchen door. But it wasn't just the handiness.

Our kids got to spend a lot of time with Lauri, as not only was she keeping our home garden but she also taught every week at the preschool, where they learned the joys of liquid seaweed, compost, and worms. As part of her curriculum, Lauri would garden and also cook with the kids—reinforcing that critical connection between garden and kitchen and making it so real, approachable, and necessary. Their lives have been forever changed for the better by the mastery Lauri brings to the subject of food and by her love of life and the earth. When we see her at the farmers market or on the street, all the kids run to her. What a joy that she has now put her love and lessons into this gorgeous book with the help of her husband, Dean, so that everyone can have Lauri and her garden wisdom in their lives.
—Suzanne Goin

Suzanne Goin is the chef and co-owner at Lucques, A.O.C., and Tavern in Los Angeles, and has earned multiple James Beard Foundation awards, including Outstanding Chef.

Above
Farmers markets are a great way
to connect with your community,
and the farmers who grow our
food are an invaluable source of
information and inspiration for our
own home gardens.

Introduction

I am nearly breathless as I reach the ninety-second step up the steep hillside. I am following Suzanne and David and their three young children to a piece of land on their property in the Santa Monica Mountains that is flat and holds the sun. The children run ahead of us, laughing, excited to explore this territory relatively far from the house and the kitchen. They ask questions. *Could there be a garden here? A place to grow food for family, friends, and possibly their restaurants? A place of secluded beauty?*

Suzanne Goin and David Lentz are two of my favorite chefs. I have eaten delicious food for many years in their celebrated restaurants Lucques, A.O.C., Tavern, and the Hungry Cat. I take a good look around. We're high up in the canyon, with no yards around, and Suzanne says she really wants the garden in the ground, not in raised beds, so it can have the feel and dignity and beauty of a farm. I check to see what kinds of trees are growing nearby and whether they might cause trouble for the garden. Eucalyptus and pine trees, for example, shed leaves and needles that can make the soil chemistry unfriendly to vegetables.

I take a seat on the ground.

The soil here is parched. It's hard to tell what it could be, given some water, good compost, and other organic amendments such as alfalfa meal and phosphate rock. I dig up some soil with my spade and put it in a bag to take with me. I sit in this spot for a while longer, tracking the arc of the sun and the westerly breeze and feel what is gorgeous about this place. I notice that there are no bees. We need bees. Without bees, a lot of the vegetables we plant will simply not produce well, and some won't produce at all. I also see some gopher holes and know that the moment we plant food, we will have many more. But I like this piece of land, so close to the California sky.

I take the bag of soil to some trusted friends: to the family-owned nursery I frequent daily and to a couple of local organic farmers whose produce is legendary. We examine the soil together. We add some water; we hold it in our hands. We decide it's good. I throw some random seeds in the ground as a test, a few kale and fava beans, water them, and come back in ten days: They have sprouted, which tells me this garden wants to grow. Then the work begins.

Below
A garden begins and ends
with a seed.

Left
Runner beans add gorgeous color
to the garden and a delicious snap
to dinner.

Compost, alfalfa meal, and more are hauled up the ninety-two steps. Citrus trees from a cherished farmer arrive; we plant those to one side. We amend, a double dig, turning earth over and folding in rich compost. Turning it back in again. African basil is the soul of my gardens, and I plant some on both sides of the plot to attract bees; its aroma is an enchantment. I let the soil rest a few days and then it's all hands in. Suzanne, David, and their kids join me in planting fava beans, lemon verbena, shiso, peas, broccoli, cauliflower, Swiss chard, purslane, and so much more. We find room for blackberries, boysenberries, golden raspberries. We water, we tend, and we grow. In time, tender pea tendrils make their way up the trellises, sunchokes reach for the sky, and arugula and other salad greens are ripe for picking. This garden surprises me with its sumptuous logic; it feels wild but there is order in this wildness—it has found its own rhythm. The outrageous colors and soul-gripping scents are as beautiful as that of any flower garden; there are wildflowers in the broccoli patch and poppies in the middle of pea shoots—no perfect rows of perfect plants here. There is food and magic bursting out onto the garden footpaths. It's like an outburst of the canyon itself.

A couple of years into the garden's growing, David is at the farmers market, and his order of sunchokes has not arrived. The restaurant's evening menu has been planned around sunchokes. He and Suzanne discuss what to do: change the menu at this late moment? Suzanne remembers that we planted sunchokes in the garden at the beginning of the season, but she's not sure how many. The blooms, which pop up high like sunflowers, had recently begun wilting. This is a sign that the sunchokes are ready to be dug up. Suzanne and David rush home and up the hillside with shovels. They begin digging, and within moments sunchokes are uncovered, a few at first and then hundreds. There are so many that friends and coworkers have to come over and help carry them down the hillside! Buried beneath the fertile ground, the handful of sunchokes we planted multiplied into enough to feed an entire community.

Edible Gardens LA

Nourishment and beauty were once separate goals for gardening, but not for me. From talking to the ever-increasing number of people who want gardens, I have learned that the combination of the two is what we really desire; not because all nourishment is beautiful in some abstract way, but because an edible garden should be as compelling to the senses as a flower or ornamental garden. This has brought a distinctive wild and connected style to my gardens that is deeply satisfying and easily achieved. *A Garden Can Be Anywhere* is a practical guide to both my personal philosophy and my essential methods for growing abundant organic food and unlocking this earthy beauty.

Suzanne and David's story perfectly illustrates the connectedness of my work: Beneath the sensory beauty of the flowers lies plentiful food and a reaffirmation of the abundance and trustworthiness of the earth, bringing families and communities together. In these pages, you will find the basic principles that guide my gardening choices:

Wildness
Formal or themed gardens feel out of touch with the natural world to me. My goal is to plant like nature plants. Plants occupy niches in the wild world thanks to sunlight, soil type, water, proximity to other plants, and more—and that's all the order we need in the garden.

Cooperation with the wild world
The garden is not isolated from nature—it is part of it. Other plants, weeds, animals, and even people are going to be in it.

Plant choice
The plants I find most essential are always changing depending on the individual whose garden I am tending, but I have a roster of regulars. African basil is a great one; I use that in every garden. The fava bean is another—I think of it as a "magic" crop.

We must let the place tell us
We learn about a place over time. The season might reveal that we mis-planted a garden, or that one item (David's sunchokes!) is a key ingredient we had previously overlooked.

Community
Beauty is made in relationships, both to the land and its inhabitants and to other people. Our families, friendships, and relationships throughout the neighborhood find expression in the garden.

Personal
Each garden is extraordinarily personal. People hire me to make gardens as an expression of their selves: their pleasures, their tastes, their desires. As the sole gardener at Edible Gardens LA, the only way I can know what the garden must be for a client is to develop a relationship to the land and interpret it. Then I plant and tend to each garden.

These principles have been born of many years' work and hundreds of gardens. Even my clients who come to me purely for the earthy and luxuriant style of my gardens soon realize that this style is the result not only of my choices, but is also an expression of themselves in cooperation with their own piece of land. I wrote this book to help people use all the lessons I have learned in order to begin a new collaboration with a unique piece of earth.

Opposite
Freshly harvested beets at the farmers market. Beets are nature's candy, sweet but also healthy. They are packed with vitamin C, folate, and magnesium.

CHAPTER ONE

A Place to Begin

Above
New garden, new beginnings.
These raised beds are made of
untreated cedar, freshly planted
for the cool season with broccoli,
kale, fava beans, Swiss chard, peas,
and plenty of herbs. Raised garden
beds should always be made from
untreated wood.

I LOVE BEGINNINGS. The start of something new gives us hope for what is possible. Beginnings harbor dreams. A garden is in a nearly constant state of beginning: turning the earth, the first seeds, the first flowers, the first harvest of a season. When I had just begun gardening, it seemed obvious that the first gesture was to focus on the soil, digging in and amending it, but after a decade in gardens I now know that the garden truly begins with the hunt for just the right place to put it.

Every week I walk into a new home, a new garden, and a new possibility. Sometimes it is easy to see where the garden will go: a bright, sunny patch just off the kitchen or an easily accessible area by a side door. But more often the ideal location for the garden is harder to find. If we're going to open up the earth, it needs to be exposed to full, all-day sun, and often that spot eludes us at first glance. Maybe there is too much shade just off the kitchen; perhaps the sunniest part of the yard is where the pool is located. When I meet with new clients, they often have a feeling about where they want the garden to go and we'll look there first: They may hope to put the garden in a little-used space at the back of the property or to bring new life to long-forgotten planters taken over by bamboo or other ornamentals. But in the end, the sun determines where the garden will go.

When assessing your outdoor space, take a walk around. Walk the back, the sides, and the front of your property, keeping an open mind about every spot.

Rule out any areas you know to be shady most of the day. Look again at the sunny spots. Sit in them for a while. Will a garden work there with your lifestyle? If there are children, can this garden coexist with the way they use the yard? How about pets or wildlife? How can the garden become a focal point or a destination where you and your family can gather? I try to find a space that is close to the kitchen or near the house in some way. For many of us, if we can't see the garden, it will be forgotten.

Sometimes the only truly sunny place is far away from the house, and that can be OK, too. This could be a destination garden (like Suzanne and David's spot high up on their hill—see page 12), a garden that beckons us to visit and that we can enhance with comforts such as an outdoor sofa or chairs to lounge and read in.

Left
A garden house in the canyon protects heirloom tomatoes and beans from critters such as opossums, raccoons, and deer.

Opposite
Landscape designer Christine London designed this tiered hillside garden, where we grow herbs such as lemon verbena, sage, chives, and parsley in abundance.

This plot of earth is "felicitious" space—a part of the home and a place for daydreams.

If there are several places that are viable for the garden, I figure in other considerations. How will you *live* with this garden? A garden is not simply a place to put plants, like a storage shed or a parking space. This plot of opened earth is what philosopher Gaston Bachelard referred to as "felicitous space"—a space, like the rest of the home, where significant events take place and with which we have a kind of poetic engagement. This is a space where we daydream, where we connect to the soil we mostly ignore elsewhere in our lives, where we are rewarded with beauty we co-create with the earth, where we begin memorable meals, and which we map in our minds as a place filled with sweet memories that we revisit in dreams. The layout of the garden, like the layout of the house, becomes embedded in our minds. For children, in particular, the garden is part of the house, which forms their first universe.

Which spot will add most to the beauty and warmth of this home? Is there space to build in a small table or seating area? If you can relax in your garden, you spend more time in your garden. The more time we spend in our gardens, the more productive and healthy they become.

Above
Putting a worktable and comfortable chairs in a greenhouse makes it an extension of the home, a place for seed-starting, a meal, or a conversation.

Opposite
Gardens bring people together—here, Lauri sets the table for friends with freshly harvested herbs and limes from the garden.

Look up and around; landscaping and trees may determine if a spot will work. Too many pine trees or eucalyptus trees can cause problems, as their needles and leaves can alter the fertility of the soil.

Many landscaping features can also impact the soil. Railroad ties, commonly used on our properties as borders or to hold back hillsides, are filled with dangerous chemicals and carcinogens. So is pressure-treated lumber designed to prevent rot and termites. The chemicals in this lumber make their way into the soil and can make an area unsafe for growing food. If there are railroad ties or other chemical concerns in the area (for instance, old lead paint chipping off a fence or the house itself), raised beds might be an option. We need to keep our food away from any source of toxins. What goes into the soil goes into our food and into our bodies.

Page 26
Queen Anne's lace and carrot flowers planted together attract pollinators and people to the garden.

Page 27
School gardens are places for learning and wonder.

Below
Harvesting lettuce, tatsoi, broccoli, and more in a garden house built to keep the deer out.

Opposite
The screen walls of a garden house are good trellises for climbers such as blackberries and peas.

The last step is to measure the actual sunlight the spot receives. A place we think of as sunny might actually be in shade for part of the day.

How to Do a Sun Study

I have an easy method for doing a sun study, and I ask my clients to follow these steps before we begin work on their garden:

1. *Take a photo of the garden space being considered every two hours between 8:00 A.M. and 4:00 P.M. It doesn't need to be done on the same day, but all days should be sunny without any clouds.*

2. *After you take a photo-graph of the area, email it to yourself with the time in the subject line. Repeat this until you have documented a full day's worth of sun hours.*

3. *When you have all the pho-tos, line them up to accu-rately determine how many hours of sun the space gets per day. Take into consid-eration the time of year. In* *the winter there will be less light and in the summer months, more. Is there going to be more or less light as you move forward in the year?*

Above
To find out how much sun a potential garden site gets per day, take a photo of that area every two hours between 8:00 A.M. and 4:00 P.M. on a sunny day.

Opposite
Place your new garden where it will get the most hours of sun per day.

Maggie's Garden

Maggie has asked me to meet with her about planting a new garden, and that means coming to her home. It means walking into her house, into her family and their place in the world. It means looking at how they live and then at the earth that lies under it all and finding the patch of dirt we'll open up to the sun, expanding their lives with new beauty. My assessment doesn't start with a square of designated dirt; it starts with Maggie waving hello at the front door.

She walks me through her modernist home and its chef's kitchen, telling me she's excited to be able to cook straight out of the garden. What's going on inside the home tells me a lot about what's going on outside; I have a good feeling she's going to use what we grow. The grounds around the house are luxuriantly landscaped, and I can see that this family is open to the wild, unpredictable communication of a garden; they're not going to hide the garden away somewhere and ignore it. They're going to make it part of their lives.

The property has a lot of outdoor space, and I start to deconstruct it—big yards surround the house, and the property is edged by all manner of decorative trees, including peppers and oaks and some huge eucalyptus trees that shade the grass. I make a note of a doorway to the lower level that might give us quick access to the house. Maggie leads me to an existing garden space no longer cultivated, somewhat remote from the house, but she wonders if it's in the wrong place. I suspect her instincts are right and I begin an assessment of the light to see where our dig should really go.

I start with the light because the vegetable garden needs sun to thrive—dark or shady places are simply not an option. When Maggie and I discuss the light and she really thinks about where she sees sun, it's not at the old garden space at the back of the property. That place is not only remote but also shaded part of the day. We realize together the garden probably needs to be moved to a side yard near the lower doorway. Once we truly consider this new spot for a while, I start taking my photos. Maggie continues the study and emails me photos throughout the day. It turns out this side yard spot has full, hot sun eight hours a day.

Opposite
Harvesting African basil, the heart of the vegetable garden. Its purple flowers draw bees to the garden site. The bees pollinate the garden as they collect nectar and pollen from all of the blossoms in the garden.

Bringing the garden closer to the kitchen begs the next question: How will the family live in this space? Who in the family intends to be active in the garden?

Plus, it is closer to the kitchen. Being close to the kitchen is handy and makes the garden part of everyday life. It is true that sometimes the only place on a property that has enough sun is actually far from the house, like a destination garden. For several of my clients, the only place that has full sun is actually the front yard, right on the street. They weren't expecting to put their garden there, in effect sharing it with the neighborhood, but it transforms those spaces and brings a new beauty to the front of the house.

Before we get too carried away with our enthusiasm for this new living space, we make a quick check of the landscaping and trees. Next to the garden spot is a small grove of decorative crape myrtle; those won't be a problem. One of Maggie's big eucalyptus trees, however, spreads its huge branches near this spot. It could shade us out, and the allelochemicals in the leaves, bark, and fragrant eucalyptus caps do have some mild negative effects on the chemistry of the garden soil. We have enough room, but she'll have to keep the tree cut back.

Above
Maggie's garden in the cool season, growing fava beans, broccoli, peas, and much more for the family table

Following Pages
Raised garden beds made from untreated cedar are placed close to the kitchen for easy harvesting.

There isn't any landscaping or hardscaping that affects the garden, such as railroad ties or quaint old outbuildings that are flaking ancient, lead-based paint. We seem to be in the clear. It's a flat space, has no problematic landscaping features, has access to water, and as far as we know has always been in grass since this house was built. She's ready to have me turn it over.

Bringing the garden closer to the kitchen begs the next question: How will Maggie's family live with this felicitous space? Who in the family intends to be active in the garden? Maggie explains that her husband is excited to be in the garden, and that they look forward to being out there with the kids. They will all be more engaged if they can see the garden from the kitchen or dining areas and can be sent out to cut a little basil or pick the fava beans when they're needed. She is pleased that the garden will bring a little wildness right in the side door and into the life of the house.

What is her idea of beautiful? She wants the color and the form and the smell of the living garden to be near her, to be part of her kids' experience of the outdoors. They have plenty of open space in the yard where they can play ball and other games, but the garden will be where they can begin to understand the beauty in the Earth and its seasons. It's also an architectural and landscape element of the property, and we talk about putting a small table and chairs outside to encourage actually living *in* the garden.

Above
One of the pleasures of the garden is eating English shelling peas fresh off the vine.

Opposite
As cabbage plants mature, young pepper seedlings sprout nearby.

Finally, we talk food! What do they want to grow?
Some families hope to grow enough food so they
rarely have to buy vegetables at the market, and
some just want a beautiful tomato or fresh greens
to supplement the daily shopping. Maggie and
her family want to grow as much as possible of
what they will eat, and this requires some room.
We decide to put in six large raised beds for a mix
of vegetables and herbs that will change with the
seasons—tomatoes, eggplant, peppers, and basil
in the warm season, and kale, chard, cabbage, fava
beans, and peas in the cool season, just to name a
few. Maggie and her family have a realistic goal, and
there is plenty of room for them to add more raised
beds to the garden if, encouraged by success, they
decide to expand. But it's already enough to produce
a lot of food! I can't be there all the time, and she and
her family will have to do some of the maintenance
and harvesting, so the garden has to be a manageable size and not feel overwhelming.

Left
Cauliflower and broccoli are
brassicas, easy-to-grow cool-
weather vegetables.

Adam's Garden

Adam asked me to come over to have a look at the house he just bought. He said there had been a rose garden just outside the kitchen, but he took the roses out before he moved in, as he wanted to grow food in that space. I was relieved not to have seen the roses, as it's emotionally hard for me, at times, to dig up what has already set down roots. But Adam had a vision for a kitchen garden. The space was bright and sunny, open to southern exposure, and I was told the flowers had done well there, so I felt confident the sun was good for vegetables. The spot was also bordered by the walls of the house on two sides, and I was concerned about any paint that had gone into the soil over the many years this house had been there, so I suggested we build raised beds.

In consultation with Adam's landscape architect, Jay Griffith, I built two long raised beds with a seating plank running along the edges so we could sit down and make harvesting and weeding easier. We moved a fountain that had been in another area of the property and placed it in the center of the two garden beds, giving it the feeling of a more traditional French garden, with the soothing sound of flowing water. Two mature citrus trees in the space were already producing large quantities of lemons and oranges, and we added some blackberries, a blood orange tree, and artichokes to expand the vegetable garden into an edible landscape.

This area of Adam's property is fairly private and would become a little refuge for him. It is not part of the regular outdoor dining and barbecue areas; it is tucked away from the lush grounds and the pool, where family and friends gather on hot summer days. It's become a place for contemplation, for thinking of meals, daydreaming, and taking control of what his family eats. It's an area for what ecopsychologist Andy Fisher calls "contact," where feelings that might not have words find their expression in the real world of dirt and rain, in pulling weeds, planting, and harvesting. All this attention to the ordinary processes of life makes the food taste better. Just like the people in our lives, our homes and the plants around them benefit from more attention. In making this area a vegetable garden, it has given new importance to the way Adam's entire property is used and how family and friends spend time here.

Opposite
We moved a fountain from another spot on Adam's property to the center of the garden, giving the space a more traditional French feel.

As Adam's house is in a canyon in Los Angeles, with lots of critters, I knew we needed to be prepared for unwanted visitors to the garden and that there was a risk we might lose more food to wildlife than Adam was able to bring into the kitchen. For these reasons, I built the garden in such a way that we could easily add fences or an enclosed structure around the area if we needed to separate it from deer, raccoons, squirrels, and all kinds of other busy nibblers. So far, we have been lucky: The worst attackers are the songbirds that like to eat the seeds we have planted into the soil. This issue is easily solved by putting a little bird netting over the plantings or starting from seedlings instead of seeds. Some of the more timid creatures such as deer are pretty wary of approaching a garden that is right up against the house, as they can see and hear the everyday living and thriving of the people who live there and they just don't want to get that close.

Adam grows vegetables for use in the kitchen, such as tomatoes, zucchini, cucumbers, and melons in the warm season and broccoli and cauliflower in the cool. I also planted my favorite, African basil, to ensure we would have plenty of bees. It makes me happy to hear the buzzing of the bees as I round the corner to the garden, hearing them before I can even see them. This is a sign of a healthy garden. The bees are vital to the production of food; they pollinate a significant percentage of our fruits and vegetables, and without them the world's supply of fresh produce would be in serious trouble. Adam understands this, and though he— like many people—was once a little fearful around bees, he now watches as they pollinate the garden, darting from one squash blossom to another, from citrus flower to melon bloom.

Above Left
Strawberries are an easy-to-grow summer treat.

Above Right
Cucumbers come in so many delicious varieties and add mystery to the garden.

Opposite
Purple podded shelling peas

Ambre's Garden

When I arrived at Ambre's home, I was greeted by her two young children. They were excited by the idea of a garden! They had been reading *Peter Rabbit* and other stories about gardens and wondered what kind of magic this new space would have in store for them. Ambre had wanted to grow food with her family for quite a long time but hadn't been able to figure out exactly where the garden should go. I took one look at the place and right away I could see why: The property near the house has small spots of sun, but most of it lies in dappled shade. The area with the most sun already had a pool. I suggested we walk the entire property together.

Ambre's home is located on a relatively flat space in the Santa Monica Mountains, but right behind the house several sets of stairs lead up the hillside. We began our ascent. At the top of the first flight of stairs is an expanse of grass and a play structure for the children; it is very sunny, but this is the only grassy area where her children can play and it didn't seem ideal for the garden, as soccer balls and baseballs were likely to end up hitting tender plants as they grew. We went up another twenty-six steps. At the top is a smaller space, but open, flat, and sunny. I was immediately drawn to this space. It is a pretty good hike from the house, but there is warmth and sun and opportunity.

Above
Ambre's garden needed to be
enclosed in order to coexist with
deer and other creatures.

We were in the middle of the mountains, so there was plenty of wildlife, too, and being so far away from the action of the house, this spot was sure to get lots of attention from opportunistic critters. Ambre confirmed that deer were regular guests up here and all around the property. Squirrels, raccoons, rats, and opossums were sure to have homes nearby as well. We would need to enclose this garden in order to live comfortably with the wildlife, so Ambre and I made a plan to build a garden house.

A garden house is similar to a greenhouse, but with screens instead of glass. The screens have openings large enough to let bees and butterflies through but keep the deer, mice, and other creatures out. In Chapter Seven, I provide all the plans and instructions you need to build one for yourself! I use a wood frame for my garden houses, and if I stain it, I make sure it ties in naturally to the surrounding area. In building Ambre's garden house, I made it as large as the flat space would allow—wide enough to hold two long garden beds. The space had water for irrigation. You will have noticed that I often use raised

garden beds; this is because we're gardening in urban areas that have been inhabited for a long time and either the soil needs a lot of amending or we're unsure about what may have been in the soil.

This fun destination garden produces lots of beautiful food for Ambre's family to enjoy. There is definitely more labor involved in bringing soil, seedlings, compost, and the like up all these stairs, but the rewards are plentiful and the children love it: A previously unused area of the property is now an exciting secret garden just like they read about in their books.

Garden Notes

1. Put your garden in the sunniest spot on the property.
2. Photograph the proposed location to confirm all-day sun.
3. Create a garden your family can live in.
4. Keep away from trees, landscaping, and structures that may cause trouble for the vegetable garden.
5. Consider the critters.
6. Plan food goals.

Above
Dinosaur kale and freshly dug fingerling potatoes from the garden

Opposite Left
The end of the season in Ambre's garden is a time of beauty and also preparation for the next planting.

Opposite Right
Purple podded peas use the sides of the garden house as a trellis.

CHAPTER TWO

Good Garden Design

GOOD GARDEN DESIGN means different things to different people. Some like a natural feel to their garden, something that has a wildness about it, while others prefer a more manicured and controlled aesthetic. Some of us have honestly never thought about it and are going to use the process of building the garden itself as a way to figure out what our own personal aesthetic is. We can be guided by our simple desire to grow food. An edible garden adds life to any landscape, demanding our attention with its butterflies and bees and its flowering stalks and vines that will produce the food we eat. We find ourselves thinking about what we will cook with those vegetables and herbs, where they are in their seasons, what care they might need. What impulse does that produce in us? An impulse to organize into neat rows? An impulse to set free in tangled vines? We suddenly discover what "beauty" means to each of us.

Left
Good design means growing for abundance, taste and even color, like this cool-season harvest of Swiss chard, broccoli, lettuce, and cauliflower.

We have already found the sunniest and best spot for our garden, so now we can look at the ways it can be built. In general, we have three options: raised beds, in the ground, and container gardening. The garden's location itself will help tell us what to do. Let's go through these options.

Opposite
Container gardening is a great way to make the most of all sunny outdoor areas. Here, blood oranges grow in abundance just next to a fountain.

Above
This garden was put in the ground in four separate plots to give its wildness a more formal structure.

Option One: Raised Beds

In my work, I find that I frequently use raised beds, and for three main reasons: They can make a garden possible where it may not have been before; they can make gardening a whole lot easier and more enjoyable; and they look great.

Raised beds allow the garden to go wherever the sun is; sometimes there is concrete or other hardscaping in the sunniest space and for these areas the only viable way to have a garden is to build raised beds to house the soil. This is also the right solution when the soil is not ideal, like hard-baked clay or pure sand, or when the soil has been compromised. Perhaps the spot was once a cinder driveway or is next to a building with flaking paint. These problems are solved by a raised bed, as the roots of your plants stay in the soil inside the bed and don't reach into the landscape below, as long as you build your beds at least 18 inches (46 cm) high.

Many people simply love the look of raised beds, which lift the garden higher into the air and make its contents more accessible and visible, and add a beautiful wood accent that can be an architectural element. Sometimes a garden that sits above the ground just looks right in the space. I personally love the look of raised beds as the wood weathers and settles in, season after season.

Left
Untreated redwood beds fade
naturally to a beautiful gray within a
year or two.

The Edible Gardens LA Guide to Building Raised Beds

Materials

Make sure to use only *untreated* wood. I cannot emphasize this enough. Wolmanized or pressure-treated wood is designed to resist rot and insects but is infused with chromium, copper, arsenic, and other chemicals, and despite industry claims that it stays in the wood and is safe, these substances have been found to leach into the soil. Similarly, do not use wood that has been stained, sealed, or painted. And even though I appreciate the sustainability benefits of reclaimed wood, don't use it in contact with garden soil, as it may have been treated with chemicals at some point. Anything that goes on or into the wood goes into the soil and into the food we eat.

For the same reasons, I don't use metal beds or beds built out of fiberglass or plastic. Occasionally a client will want beds built out of raw steel or even galvanized steel because they like the way it looks, but those metals do leach into the soil, particularly the zinc used in galvanizing. Similarly, some plastics and fiberglass leach chemicals into water and soil.

Above
Dahlias are a welcome addition to the vegetable beds.

Opposite
Garden beds can be built on a properly tiered hillside.

Building

I recommend building beds 18 to 24 inches (46 to 61 cm) high.

Build beds any length you desire, but don't build them wider than 4 feet (1.2 m), as it becomes too difficult to reach into the middle of the beds to tend vegetables or amend soil. As a rule, the beds I build are between 3 and 4 feet (.9 and 1.2 m) wide.

The bottom of the bed is open to the ground below, so if you live in an area with gophers, be sure to line the bottom of your garden beds with gopher wire.

Above
A little planning lets us maximize the amount of space we can give to a new garden.

Opposite Top Left
Longer garden beds require a brace or two in the middle to keep the beds from bowing.

Opposite Top Right
Place garden beds a minimum of 2 feet (61 cm) apart to allow for easy movement between the beds.

Opposite Bottom Left
Mid-installation, making sure the new garden beds are properly aligned

Opposite Bottom Right
Once gopher wire is installed at the bottom of the garden beds and irrigation piping is in place, it's time to fill the beds with good organic soil.

The Architectural Touch

If you wish to tie the garden beds in to the aesthetic of your home, you can build a bed inside a bed, or front the beds with other materials. For instance, if you want the bed to be painted or stained or made with reclaimed wood, you can use these materials to build a secondary garden bed over the actual untreated-wood raised bed. Think of it as a shell. None of the reclaimed or painted wood will touch the soil that the food is being grown in; it will go on the outside of the raised garden beds. Be sure to leave 2 to 3 inches (5 to 7.5 cm) of breathing room between the aesthetic layer and the actual garden beds to allow for the expansion and swelling of the wood.

Soil

Once the garden beds are built and irrigation lines placed (we will discuss irrigation in detail in Chapter Four), fill the beds with rich organic soil. Keep it local by finding a producer of organic soils and compost in your region, if possible. Leave 1 to 2 inches (2.5 to 5 cm) at the top of each garden bed and add organic compost. I find that putting a layer of compost at the top makes seed-starting easier and helps feed the soil every time the garden is watered.

Plans for an Edible Gardens LA Raised Garden Bed

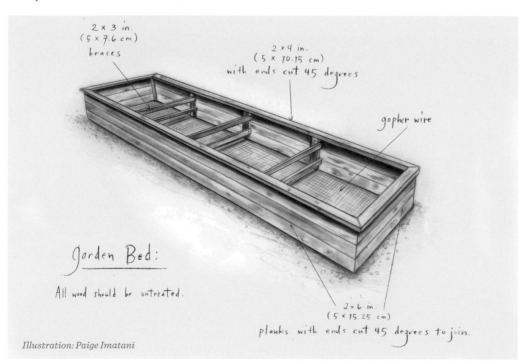

2 x 3 in.
(5 x 7.6 cm)
braces

2 x 4 in.
(5 x 10.15 cm)
with ends cut 45 degrees

gopher wire

Garden Bed:

All wood should be untreated.

2 x 6 in.
(5 x 15.25 cm)
planks with ends cut 45 degrees to join.

Illustration: Paige Imatani

Opposite
Good soil is everything. It is a gardener's canvas, on which the art of the garden takes shape. The soil holds the story of our gardens, ever changing and evolving.

Above Left
Placing the African basil in a corner between beds ensures that bees will find their way to the garden as the highly fragrant flowers bloom.

Above Right
A garden is a place to rest and restore both the mind and body. This is the same garden, only a month or so after planting.

Option Two: In the Ground

The classic garden experience is to turn up and amend the soil underfoot and put the plants directly in the ground. This connects your food directly to the terroir of the place, which means it takes up the flavors and character of the soil with its minerals and micronutrients. Every spot adds different flavor notes to the food. Growing food in the ground, without the use of raised beds, reduces the cost and time required to start a vegetable garden because there's less construction to do. I enjoy both methods of growing and am inspired by the possibilities of both designs.

At the Esalen Institute in Big Sur, California, one of my favorite kitchen gardens, the vegetables are planted directly in the earth in long rows on a bluff overlooking the ocean. All day the plants are bathed in hot Pacific sun and slightly salty sea mist. These things affect the vegetables. The ends of each row are bursting with seasonal flowers, and the rows themselves abound with well-tended and much-loved produce that is used in the kitchen and served to the staff and guests of Esalen. The institute's commitment to the land and to the building of rich organic soil is apparent in the bounty, beauty, and delicious taste of the produce that comes from their garden.

If planting your garden directly in the ground is most appealing to you, I recommend using the double dig method to amend the soil. The double dig was made popular by John Jeavons, a leader in the field of biointensive agriculture.

Below
Harvesting chard at Chase Farm in Maine. Planting directly in the ground pulls the flavors of the place into the produce.

Opposite
I have been marveling at the organic gardens at Esalen in Big Sur for years, watching how they feed both the guests and the surrounding community. The orange flowering medicinal herb lion's tail anchors the vegetable beds.

Double Dig

Before You Dig

Begin by marking off the area you have chosen for your garden with found stones or stakes. As with raised beds, I recommend planning for a width of no more than 4 feet (1.2m) and then as long as desired—8, 15, 20 feet (2.4, 4.6, 6.1 m) or more. Next, remove all the weeds and grass using a garden fork to loosen the soil and make weed removal easy. If there is sod, take off that layer.

1

Select a shovel with a blade about 1 foot (30.5 cm) long, and a wheelbarrow or buckets or a garden tarp to catch the dirt. Begin at one end of the garden space and stomp the shovel in up to the top of the blade or one shovel-length deep.

2

Take that soil out and place it aside or in the wheelbarrow or tarp. Turning the soil over reveals plant roots that need to be removed from the garden.

3

Take the trench down to a depth equal to at least one length of the shovel blade (about 12 inches [30.5 cm]), and preferably two lengths (24 inches or 61 cm), to make room for compost.

4

Once your first trench is done, fill it one shovel-length deep with compost. Adding fresh compost to the garden brings new life to the soil.

5

Lay fresh layers of compost down each of the rows.

6

Once the fresh compost is placed in the trench, cover it with a layer of the existing soil.

7

With that row finished, lay out your next trench right alongside the first one. As you're digging the new trench, use the soil to fill in the original trench until it is just about full again. I like to add an additional layer of compost to the top.

8

Repeat these steps until the garden area has been completely amended. Because you are adding lots of compost, you may have soil left over at the end. If this method still feels confusing, there are excellent videos of the double dig method online that can give you a visual tutorial. When the entire area has been amended via a double dig, you are ready to plant.

My version of the double dig method requires a shovel, good compost, and a bit of muscle.

Option Three: Container Gardens

For many years, I had a large, flat area of land where I could grow my vegetables directly in the ground. But then I moved into a house in a wooded and secluded canyon with steep hillsides and soil that had been compromised by the use of creosote-soaked railroad ties. I looked at this as an opportunity to learn more about container gardening. I was shocked by how much food and beauty can be grown in big pots!

In large terra-cotta pots, wooden containers, ceramic pots, and half barrels, I planted fruit trees including pomegranate, fig, peach, plum, raspberries, apple, blood orange, Meyer lemon, and more. The results have been spectacular, with fresh fruit right outside our door many months of the year. I also started growing vegetables and herbs in large raised planter beds on the brick patios. This has become one of my favorite ways to garden, as it puts herbs and vegetables that my family uses daily within easy reach of the kitchen while we cook.

Above
Hand-built enclosed planters
are critter-proof and beautiful
on the patio.

Opposite
Broccoli thrives in a deep pot with
plenty of room for roots to grow.

Following Pages
In a landscape designed by
Matthew Brown, we planted blood
orange, peach, and plum trees in large
terra-cotta pots.

Container gardening allows us to create a garden anywhere, as long as there is ample sunshine and structural integrity to hold the weight: on a patio, next to a pool, on top of a retaining wall, on a balcony, on a roof. When planning your container garden, be sure to use containers that are deep enough for healthy root growth. For example, when looking to grow tomatoes in a pot, the container should be as tall as your knee, as the roots need 18 to 24 inches (46 to 61 cm) to feed deep into the soil. Vegetables such as peas and beans don't root as deeply, so they can be in a pot only 1 foot (30.5 cm) deep. Here is a chart showing how deep your containers need to be for some common plantings:

HOW DEEP SHOULD THE POTS BE?

7 to 8 inch (18 to 20 cm)
Herbs such as
thyme, oregano, sage, mint

12 inch (30.5 cm)
Vegetables and herbs including
kale, Swiss chard, peas, cucumbers, beans, lettuce, arugula, collards, basil, radishes, spinach, chamomile, anise hyssop, chervil, cumin, chives, epazote, lemon balm, marjoram, lovage, parsley, cilantro, rosemary, shiso

18 inch (46 cm)
Vegetables including
tomatoes, tomatillos, peppers, fennel, broccoli, cauliflower, beets, cabbage, eggplant, onions, leeks

Feel free to mix and match different kinds of containers that appeal to you, as long as they are not made of plastic, fiberglass, or wood that is painted or stained. Just like with raised beds, keep in mind that whatever your containers are made of goes into your food. Use ceramic, stone, or untreated-wood containers. Be sure to consult with a builder or structural engineer before putting heavy pots on decks or roofs to be certain they can hold the weight. After watering, they can become even heavier.

Fill containers with rich, organic potting soil and use a thin layer of compost at the top to prepare pots for planting.

Above
Sage and many other herbs grow nicely in pots 7 to 8 inches (18–20 cm) deep.

Opposite
Purple cauliflower needs a pot 18 inches (46 cm) deep. It adds a burst of color to the garden and the plate.

A Backyard with Raised Garden Beds

Blair and David wanted a vegetable garden that would help them eat healthier and also introduce their young daughter to just how our food is grown. Though they had little experience with gardening, they were all excited to jump in and learn. When we talked about the design and size of their garden, Blair and David wanted a garden that would encourage more outdoor time, be easily accessible to the kitchen, and feel very user-friendly.

I didn't want them to be overwhelmed by starting off too big, so we dedicated a portion of their backyard to growing food with the understanding that we could build it out further as time went by. The yard has flat terrain and plenty of sun, and for this family, using raised beds felt like the best choice, as they would make gardening easier and tie in well with their beautifully landscaped home. We built four raised beds of equal size, each 3 by 12 feet (.9 by 3.7 m), made from untreated redwood. They are 18 inches (46 cm) high to support healthy root growth. The garden beds are arranged in two rows with 3 feet (91 cm) left free between the ends of each bed and 3 feet (91 cm) between the rows. This allows plenty of room to move through the garden even at the height of the season, when the stems and vines are bursting from every edge. You can zigzag in between the four beds instead of having to walk 24 feet (7.3 m) in order to go around the end of a bed. I also really like breaking up long garden beds simply because it makes the garden look better; extremely long planks of wood don't feel natural in every setting.

We filled the garden beds with good organic soil, topped them with compost, and planted the first seeds. It takes time and experience to figure out how far apart the seeds and seedlings should go, and the first season we got a little overzealous planting Zucchino Rampicante squash, and it turned into a squash explosion! There was more zucchini than the residents of their entire street could consume. Time in the garden teaches us all about balance in nature and in life. We now grow generous amounts of all kinds of vegetables in this garden and are careful to leave room for new varieties as well. In the warm season, there are eggplant, shishito peppers, Green Zebra and Momotaro tomatoes, squash, parsley, cucumbers, basil, and more. In the cool season, favorites include kale, onions, radishes, broccoli, and lettuce.

Right
A garden creates life and possibility where there was only lawn or pavers before.

Below
Flowers and vegetables mingle seamlessly within the garden beds.

Opposite
Blair and David's vegetable garden, placed close to the house, extends the living space of the home as it beckons us outdoors.

Following Page Left
Everyone in the household enjoys picking fresh chard from the garden.

Following Page Right
Freshly harvested lettuce for the evening meal in a bowl made by ceramicist Victoria Morris

A Garden Within a Garden

Chona and her family are passionate about food. Chona is a natural cook and makes mealtime an important and delicious component of family life. I taught gardening to both of her children in one of the school gardens where I teach, and she could see that they became more adventurous eaters when they understood the connection between the food on their plates and how it got there. When the time came for them to move into a new home, Chona asked me to help with an edible garden. Working with the Los Angeles–based architecture firm Marmol Radziner, they built their beautiful new home from the ground up and used reclaimed ski fencing for the siding.

Marmol Radziner designed a wonderful space for the edible garden and wanted to tie the reclaimed ski siding of the home in to the actual garden beds. I explained my concerns about possible chemicals from the fencing leaching into the soil and suggested building an interior garden bed made from untreated wood with an exterior garden bed made of the same reclaimed ski fencing that was on the house. This is what I refer to as a "garden within a garden." As long as a 2- to 3-inch (5- to 7.5-cm) space is left between the inner and outer garden bed materials, the garden beds will thrive and have plenty

of room for the natural expansion of the wood. This way, the soil inside is never compromised by any chemicals from the decorative ski fencing on the outside. The beds were built with this garden-within-a-garden design and then we filled them with rich organic soil and compost. A drip system was put in place to help ensure the beds receive ample water, and then the fun of planting began.

The first season, this family wanted to try making pickles and we grew cucumbers of many kinds: Persian, lemon, Japanese, Armenian, and more! We continue to grow cucumbers as well as mustard greens, hot peppers including Thai chilies and purple jalapeños, and big, juicy tomatoes such as Aunt Ginny's, Pineapple, Ananas Noire, and Black Krim. This is a garden for all the senses, with a large herb section and flowers that include Black Swan poppies, sweet peas, and yarrow. It sits beside the pool and just outside the kitchen. The garden is an integral part of everyday life for Chona and her family.

Opposite
Chona's garden beds use reclaimed ski fencing on the exterior. The fencing wraps around beds made of untreated wood to ensure soil safety. Landscape design by Marmol Radziner

Below
I planted strawberries along the edges of the herb bed, which also includes oregano, cilantro, rosemary, basil, and marjoram.

French-Style Symmetry in an In-Ground Garden

Jody has a wonderful garden that is the centerpiece of her home. It is in a sunny area in the courtyard. Her home has large glass doors and windows and the garden is visible from almost every room in the house.

Jody's garden, designed by Christine London, is in the style of a four-quadrant French garden: There are four garden squares of equal width and a potted apple tree in the center of each square. It is a beautifully constructed space and influenced the choices I made when deciding which vegetables, flowers, and herbs to grow there. The symmetry seems to add to the order and structure of the home, while the plants and flowers that burst from these squares show that life wants to spill out and fill the place with wildness. It's a nice balance.

This garden is a very special place to be. There are additional fruit trees growing nearby including lemon, lime, and pomegranate. Gravel walkways run in between the square, in-ground garden plots, allowing you to stroll through and giving you a place to sit while working in the garden. Her garden beds are gently amended with compost each new season to keep the soil healthy and strong. We grow whatever is in season, and some of her favorites are yellow straightneck squash, Aunt Ginny's tomatoes, Rosa Bianca eggplant, and lemon basil. Of course, we add lots of flowers and flowering herbs to bring the bees. Favorite flowers here include Bee's Friend, cosmos, borage, and Bachelor Button.

Opposite Above
Potted apple trees anchor all four quadrants in Jody's garden, designed by Christine London. Apple trees come in many varieties with different chill-hour requirements (some trees need a number of hours in cooler temperatures in order to produce). Find the best variety for where you live.

Opposite Below
Squash blossoms open in the early morning hours and close as the day warms.

Following Pages
Jody's garden is in a courtyard visible from much of the house, thus inviting the outside in. I like interplanting fava beans, broccoli, poppies, squash, green beans, radishes, and kale.

Container Gardening in the Canyon

Container gardening can be a very beautiful and easy way to garden. It is also ideal for balconies, decks, and even rooftops. As mentioned earlier, always be sure to have a licensed professional work on weight-bearing guidelines for any of these areas. I also like to use containers around pools or any area of the home that is hardscaped.

In my own home, I wanted to create an outdoor dining area on my deck with an abundance of fruit trees and potted herbs. My family lives in a heavily wooded canyon, and an enormous oak tree grows just next to the deck and hangs over it; hot sun filters through this tree all afternoon. A wonderful, round wood dining table anchors the center of the deck. I wanted to eat in a garden of trees and so I

planted figs, apples, blackberries, pomegranates, peaches, plums, lemons, limes, and oranges in pots circling the eating area. I love spending time with my family and friends at this table, eating delicious food while surrounded by the fragrance of citrus blossoms and the beauty of flowering stone fruit. Often when my husband and I are cooking dinner, one of us will go out to the deck to gather rosemary, sage, thyme, and basil for the meal we are preparing.

A garden can be anywhere. We just need to find the method that works the best for our own land and our personal food and lifestyle goals.

Garden Notes

1. Determine the garden type that best suits your space:

   Raised beds

   Good for hardscape or compromised soil

   Make gardening easy on the back

   Look great

   In the ground

   Least expensive

   Direct connection to soil flavors

   Container gardens

   Good for small spaces on decks, roofs, patios

2. Pay careful attention to what landscape materials are used in your outdoor area to decide which garden design type is best.

3. Take your cues from nature: How will this garden add to the beauty of the buildings, trees and shrubs, and terrain that already exist there?

Above
A beautiful vegetable garden makes the whole landscape more dynamic.

Opposite Left
You can grow a lot of delicious fruit in just a few large pots.

Opposite Right
Tomato blossoms add a grace note of garden color.

CHAPTER THREE

The Story Is in the Soil

Working the Earth

OUR HEARTS LEAP when we see rich, dark, fertile earth. We know when it's good or not. It tugs at something old within us, creatures who've made our living for the last five to ten thousand years coaxing plants out of the ground. That beautiful, spongy texture, the promise of life within it. This deep attraction never ceases to be a source of joy and wonder; a connection to the earth is *in* us.

One of the most satisfying experiences I have, as a gardener, is to dig up a relatively barren plot of land—say, a patch of alluvial clay hardened for years in someone's backyard—and to turn it, to reintroduce it to air and water, to soften it and feed it with rich compost and animal manures and minerals, to see it slowly fill with humus and soil life. It is a joy to watch it change season after season as the crops in it improve, from struggling beans and peas, which fix nitrogen in the soil, to the best-tasting spinach or chard you've ever eaten in your life. I have to admit that this kind of total restoration is thrilling—but why? Why does healthy soil make us feel so good? There's more to it than delicious spinach. The story in the soil is about much more than just what we put in and what we take out.

The most important thing that we grow in the ground is our relationship to the living soil itself. The soil, like the oceans or the sky above our heads, is a complex, living superorganism. It teems with life! When soil is healthy, it is a wild riot of plants, fungi, microorganisms such as bacteria, protozoa, and algae, invertebrates such as worms, and all manner of insects and tiny insect-like critters such as springtails and mites, plus relative giants like rodents and toads. Consider for a moment just the fungi alone: There can be yards and yards of beneficial threadlike fungal filaments growing in a thimbleful of soil. That same gram of soil could contain a *billion* helpful bacteria. The top 5 inches (13 cm) of an acre of topsoil can contain anywhere from 124 to 425 *million* insects!

It takes a huge amount of communication to keep all that flora and fauna healthy, and when we work to that end, we are part of a grand dialogue. This wild discourse is what I love most about gardening, and so often it happens without us even knowing it. Don't worry about it being too complex—we were literally born into this relationship! We, too, are creatures made of this Earth. If we do our part, the soil tells us what it needs so that all this bustling life can flourish.

Above
Freshly harvested celery

Opposite
Swiss chard is a workhorse of the garden. It will grow and continue to produce from one season to the next.

A GARDEN CAN BE ANYWHERE

Below
Bees are a garden's best friend.
Without bees, many of the garden
plants will simply fail to thrive.

Opposite
Worms make for healthy soil. Their
castings feed the soil, and the tunnels
they make improve soil structure,
keeping the soil aerated and able to
hold water more efficiently.

To borrow a thought from fellow gardener John Jeavons, we should stop growing crops and start growing soil. Jeavons is a gardening pioneer whose book *How to Grow More Vegetables* I've used as a vital reference for years. "Growing soil" requires that we shift our perspective: We don't just pour nutrients into the dirt and haul out the crops, looking to minimize the input and maximize the output. Instead, we live in *relation* to the dirt under our feet, talking back and forth with it in the form of food and nutrients and water and waste and pH and beetles and lizards and countless other indicators.

If we can get this communication right, not only do we grow more and healthier food, but we foster a better biotic community for every living thing, preserve topsoil that is otherwise rapidly diminishing, and create a more sustainable human culture. As celebrated British organic farming pioneer Sir Albert Howard said, "The health of soil, plant, animal and man is one and indivisible."

In effect, your whole garden functions as one holistic organism, and as wielders of the trowel and eaters of the juicy peaches, you and your family are central figures in it. It all begins with soil. The soil is everything.

I build and maintain organic gardens, and I won't grow any other way. There are several organic growing methods that have been baptized with their own names, such as biodynamics and Jeavons's Grow Biointensive, but they are all based on growing healthy soil. The term "organic" has at least two different common meanings, and both have to do with our communication with the soil. The first is when we see food marked as "organic" in the market: That means it has been grown without fertilizers made in a chemical factory and it has not been treated with chemical pesticides, insecticides, or fungicides. Those fertilizers are industrial salts, and all those "-cides" are poisons by definition and shouldn't be anywhere near your food. A lot of them require special genetically modified plants designed to grow in the poison environment they create.

Left
With Alex Weiser of Weiser Family Farms and the Tehachapi Heritage Grain Project. An inspiring and prolific farmer

But there's a second, deeper meaning to "organic" that is about much more than just skipping the chemicals. It's about what we add to the soil instead. Organic gardening means constantly building the soil by increasing the organic material in it. We are seeking to build humus, which is cured organic material (meaning it has decomposed and dried six months). We do this by adding compost—composting is the simple key to a great garden! This material, unlike chemical fertilizers, is made up of decayed plant and animal matter and waste such as manure. In other words, the stuff that has created soil since the dawn of time. It contains most of the nutrition and minerals the garden needs, plus other essentials such as mycorrhiza (the tiny fungal threads that help the garden communicate and distribute nutrients). The humus created in the garden makes better soil structure by increasing the amount of fluff or air in the soil (great soil is about 50 percent air by volume), thus allowing the fine root hairs of the plants to penetrate easily in all directions. Humus is also food, and a critical part of the food chain for all the microbial life, worms, insects, and the like that support plant growth.

When you learn to protect the soil, you'll discover that this profound and grand relationship produces another crop: joy. You'll feel joy at knowing that this patch of earth is alive and flourishing, and you'll be rewarded with gorgeous food you can share. This joy is the leap we feel in our hearts when we see beautiful soil. The healthier it is, the healthier we can be.

Above
Nothing says summer like ripe and juicy fruit.

Opposite
Tatsoi, an Asian green and one of my favorites, is similar in flavor to spinach.

If you are planting your garden directly in the ground, you are going to need to determine what type of soil you have. To do this, begin by watering it and then waiting a day or two. Then pick up a handful of the soil. You can know so much about soil just by holding it in your hand. If you squeeze a handful of soil and then open your hand and it sifts off like sand, it doesn't have much structure. We call that sandy soil. Alternatively, if it stays stuck together even when you poke it with the fingers of your other hand, that's also not so good. We refer to that as clay soil. Good soil should break apart into small lumps, or be "friable," containing lots of air but held together by fungal filaments, root sugars, and the sticky product of bacteria breaking down humus, which is called glomalin.

Whether you have sandy soil or clay soil or just soil that has been waiting to be tended to and loved, you are going to begin amending the soil by opening up the earth. I use the double dig method discussed in the previous chapter. During that process, I amend with a rich organic compost. Compost is a gardener's best friend. It nurtures the soil. Compost provides much-needed organic matter to both clay and sandy soils and feeds all soil with nutrients and life! It is used when first planting a garden, during the growing season, and for amending the plot of land from one season to the next. Starting the garden with a simple amending of compost starts you on an organic process and ensures a fair amount of success with your first crop.

If you do not yet have an active compost pile, it is best to begin by using either well-aged horse manure from nearby stables or an organic compost made by a reputable company. I like Bu's Blend from the Malibu Compost Company and both types of compost from the Vermont Compost Company.

You can also look to your local independent nursery to find locally produced organic compost.

How Much Compost to Use?

For a 4 by 8 foot (1.2 by 2.4 m) garden bed, plan on using three bags of compost that measure 1 cubic foot per bag. For a 4 by 16 foot (1.2 by 4.9 m) garden bed, use six bags. Over time, you will get a better sense of how much compost your garden needs; sometimes it will be a little more, sometimes a bit less, depending on the vegetables grown. It's good to keep a couple of bags of compost on hand to use as needed.

Amending Raised Beds

If you are working with a raised bed garden, the first season is very simple. You will fill the raised beds with organic soil and put a couple of inches of compost at the top.

After the first season, you will need to amend the garden beds for the new season to give the soil a vital boost of nutrition. To do this, dig down to the bottom of the beds and turn the soil over, removing all roots and leaving just loose soil in the beds. Then, just as you would with a garden that is directly in the ground, dig a shovel-length deep and a shovel-width wide into the soil, working down a row, and move the soil to the side. Add compost, a shovelful at a time, working back down that same row. Like we did in the double dig, continue layering the old soil and the compost.

Above
Making your own compost is easy and an important way to return household wastes back to the garden.

Opposite
Good friable soil should clump together slightly when you squeeze it, but not stay packed together like clay. It should be loose so it can hold a lot of water and air.

Additional Soil Amendments for Both In-the-Ground and Raised Beds

As you amend your vegetable garden patch or raised bed garden with compost, you are going to want to add a few additional soil amendments to give back to the soil what it has given out to the plants that were grown the previous season. Soil tests will tell you which amendments your soil needs, but I admit I don't often do the laboratory tests. I try to take my cues from the plants themselves. I do lab tests only if the plants just don't respond to regular nutrition. I like to use a combination of rock phosphate (for phosphorus and calcium), alfalfa meal (for nitrogen, phosphorus, potassium, magnesium and sulfur), greensand (for potassium, iron, and magnesium), kelp meal (for potassium), and colloidal phosphate and azomite (for trace minerals). You probably don't need to add nitrogen; the good compost that you are using to amend the garden beds is providing plenty of vital nitrogen for the soil and plants.

To properly test the soil, you can get a professional soil test to determine what nutrients are missing from your soil and how much you need to add. Local soil labs can generally handle this, and often the agricultural extension programs at your state colleges do it, too. If you have concerns about environmental hazards such as lead paint (from a fence or house), or if you are starting a garden near a high-traffic area such as a highway or near a coal-fired power plant, gas station, or commercial building, I absolutely recommend soil testing be done. I want to reiterate that edibles should never be planted near any kind of treated lumber.

Once the soil has been amended, water it daily and let it sit for a couple of days, which allows the freshly amended soil to settle. Now the garden can be planted. (See Chapter Five for planting strategies.)

Below Left
Amending gardens with fresh compost is the best way to prepare for a new growing season.

Below Right
Interplanting pea seeds in the broccoli and cauliflower patch. Peas add nitrogen to the soil as they grow, enriching the soil for heavy nitrogen feeders like broccoli and cauliflower.

Opposite
Artichokes are beautiful as food and as form.

Making your own compost is easy and an important way to return household wastes back to the garden. Some people worry that it will attract pests or be a bit smelly, but done well, there is no need for concern.

Compost is made by taking kitchen scraps such as carrot tops, banana peels, coffee grounds, and the like and mixing them with things such as dead leaves, shredded newspaper, and ripped-up brown mailing boxes. Think of it as "green" (nitrogen) and "brown" (carbon). That is all it is—the green and the brown cut, shredded, or ripped into smaller pieces and put together in a bin. This bin is referred to as the compost pile. You will see "recipes" for ratios of brown and green matter, but I have found that just using what you have on hand and mixing it all up together works really well. I water and turn my compost over once or twice a week to help it "cook." That is the magic: The heat created by the decomposing green and brown makes compost. Your bin can be held neatly in a plastic tumbler made specifically for compost, or you can build a wooden frame box to hold it. In either case, your first batch of compost will require some patience, as it can take nearly a year for that first batch to decompose, cook, and turn into beautiful soil for your garden. After the first batch is ready, always leave a couple of shovelfuls in the composter or pile to help activate the next batch. You can buy organic compost starters, which can be added to the pile a couple of times a year to help move the process along. Adding alfalfa to the compost pile also helps it mature. Never use meats, dairy, or processed foods in the compost pile. I also avoid onions and citrus in the compost pile.

SOME DOS AND DON'TS FOR THE COMPOST PILE

Do add:

1. *Fruit and vegetable scraps: peels, tops, etc.*
2. *Eggshells*
3. *Coffee grounds*
4. *Grass clippings*
5. *Leaves*
6. *Newspapers*
7. *Brown mailing boxes*

Don't add:

1. *Diseased plants*
2. *Meats*
3. *Dairy*
4. *Processed foods*

Above
Placing the compost bin close to the vegetable beds makes for easy use.

Opposite
Composting bins made from untreated redwood

Understanding NPK

When we talk about soil fertility, we're generally talking about three vital macronutrients that all plants draw from the soil: nitrogen (N), phosphorus (P), and potassium (K). There are many other minerals that are important to plant life, including sulfur, magnesium, and calcium, but N, P, and K are the nutrients depleted most by growing crops. To add nutrients beyond what is in compost, we add fertilizers. You will see an NPK rating listed on most soil fertilizers, both organic and nonorganic, usually as a series of numbers, such as 7-5-5. That means that, for every 100 parts of the product, 7 are nitrogen, 5 are phosphorus, and 5 are potassium. Those numbers are important because sometimes you want to pour on the nitrogen, so you pick a fertilizer with a high "N" number, and sometimes you need a blast of potassium, so you pick a fertilizer with a high "K" number. I will walk you through those circumstances below.

I fertilize using only organic fertilizers. Like matured manure or compost, these are made from decaying or digested organic matter—generally plant material. Commercial organic fertilizers are marked with NPK numbers. My favorite organic fertilizer is liquid seaweed, which is organic and made from kelp. It is nature's plant supercharger! It has what the garden needs; nitrogen, magnesium, zinc, iron and potassium. I use it every two weeks, diluting it with water in a large watering can and then watering both the soil and the leaves of the plant, giving them a good foliar feeding.

At one time, I used commercial fish emulsion as a fertilizer, because I believed the material in it was a good use of fish by-products. I have since learned that the fish in many fish meal and fish emulsion products are netted specifically for this purpose, to the detriment of other ocean life. Liquid seaweed or kelp, on the other hand, is sustainable.

Nonorganic fertilizers come in convenient pellet forms, but I stay away from them for all the reasons I laid out at the beginning of this chapter. Plus, they are salts, and as they dissolve they acidify the soil, lowering the pH, which then has to be addressed with lime or some other additive. Worst of all, the nitrogen and phosphorus in nonorganic fertilizers are generally made using petroleum products, and I don't want to encourage pulling more fossil fuels out of the ground.

EACH ELEMENT HAS A DIFFERENT FUNCTION:
Nitrogen: green growth
Phosphorus: flower, fruit, and root growth
Potassium: stem strength

HERE IS MY SHORT LIST OF THE MATERIALS I USE TO SUPPLY THESE NUTRIENTS:
Nitrogen (N)
1. *Compost*
2. *Aged/composted animal manures such as cow, horse, chicken (never fresh due to pathogens)*

Phosphorus (P)
3. *Soft rock phosphate*
4. *Colloidal phosphate*

Potassium (K)
5. *Greensand*
6. *Azomite*
7. *Kelp meal*

Trace Minerals
8. *Liquid seaweed*
9. *Alfalfa meal*

Opposite
A harvest of kale, tatsoi, and edible borage flowers

Page 106
Planting cherry tomatoes and other small tomato varieties ensures an early harvest while waiting for heirlooms and other large tomatoes to mature.

Page 107
Cosmos and borage flowers are beautiful additions to the tomato bed.

Unless I have done a soil test that clearly shows the garden is missing some key nutrient, I start off a new garden with only compost and, once every two weeks, liquid seaweed diluted in water. That generally does the trick. After the initial growing season, however, I gently amend the garden with compost again and add nutrients such as soft rock phosphate or alfalfa meal(for phosphorus), greensand (for potassium), and colloidal phosphate (for calcium, trace minerals, and phosphorus) to prepare the soil for the next season.

When to Add Extra Nutrients and Minerals

Some of our garden plants can benefit from an extra boost of nitrogen, phosphorus, or potassium during the growing season. Adding these at just the right time can really kick your garden into high gear. Tomatoes, for instance, which thrive in the hot weather, really do well with an infusion of nitrogen when they're planted as seeds or seedlings, so I give them a regular feeding of diluted liquid seaweed. And later, when the plants are established and almost flowering, I give them a boost of potassium, such as kelp meal, to help them produce delicious fruit. I also add calcium in the form of ground-up eggshells when I am preparing the planting bed for the tomatoes to help support their growth and delicious taste.

Not all plants are the same, of course, but many plants can do better with this kind of simple nutrient boost. Beets, for example, do well when you add some extra phosphorus, such as soft rock phosphate or alfalfa meal, to the soil where they will be planted. In fact, all root vegetables, such as parsnips, carrots, rutabagas, and onions, thrive when the soil where they will be grown is fed with extra phosphorus.

Once the garden is prepared for the growing season and the season's first crops have been harvested, it's time to use plant rotation to keep the soil healthy. "Rotating" the plants simply means switching out which plants are grown in each spot in the garden. For example, you don't want to grow tomatoes in the same spot year after year, as the soil will rapidly deplete and plants will be more prone to soil-borne diseases. My method is fairly simple: I rotate plants that use high amounts of nitrogen with plants that bring nitrogen back into the soil. Here are some examples:

After I grow tomatoes, I grow fava beans the following season. Fava beans, like all legumes, pull nitrogen out of the air and "fix" it in the soil into a form that can be used by other plants.

After I grow beans, I grow eggplant. Eggplant uses that stored nitrogen.

After I grow eggplant, I grow peas. The peas fix nitrogen again.

After I grow peas, I grow corn, which uses the nitrogen.

And so on.

These are just a few examples. Here is a list of popular vegetables broken down into crops that use more nitrogen and those that use less. Rotating high-demand and low-demand vegetables ensures good soil health.

ROTATE HIGHER- AND
LOWER-DEMAND PLANTS

Higher Demand for Nitrogen

Eggplant

Tomatoes

Corn

Squash

Cucumbers

Cabbage

Lower Demand for Nitrogen

Peas

Beans

Fava beans

Carrots

Crop rotation is absolutely essential to create and keep good soil health. Create a list of the foods you want to grow and then determine their feeding demands. The nitrogen needs of crops not on my chart here are readily available online. If your garden has just one bed, give the soil a very robust amendment before the growing season and be sure to add some extra compost during the growing season. Also, try to move those high-demand plants around as much as possible each season to prevent the soil from depleting and affecting the viability and health of the crops.

Healthy soil doesn't happen overnight and it can take several years to bring soil into good health. Many soils have received little or no nourishment for years and it takes time to replenish what has been lost. Crop rotation helps to establish soil health faster and to maintain it once it is achieved.

Opposite Top Left

Cherry tomatoes can bring early and heavy harvests.

Opposite Top Right

Eggplants are nitrogen users, so after this harvest we will plant beans or another nitrogen fixer to restore nutrition to the soil.

Opposite Bottom Left

Members of the Brassica family, such as cauliflower, collard greens, and broccoli, all benefit from being planted where summer beans were grown.

Opposite Bottom Right

Follow summer sweet corn with peas or fava beans to restore nitrogen to the soil.

Soil pH

You could garden for years and never measure the pH of the soil, and if you're getting good results then there's probably no reason to do it. It's one of those things you measure if you suspect there's a problem. The letters "pH" stand for "potential hydrogen," and pH measures whether the soil's liquid content, or soil water, is acidic or alkaline. In soil, the numbers on the pH scale generally run from 4, which is acidic, to 8.5, which is alkaline, or basic. A measure of 7 is neutral. Gardens tend to grow best in slightly acidic soil, as naturally occurring acids such as humic acid and carbonic acid aid the breakdown of some nutrients in humus and make them easier for plants to use. A soil pH of anywhere from 6 to 7 is generally very good.

If you do find that your soil is too acidic, you can add lime—a processed type of limestone, which is alkaline—to lower the acidity of your soil. Lime is available at local nurseries. Plan on adding lime to your garden beds every four years. Lime also helps the garden by adding calcium to the soil.

Opposite
A soil pH between 6 and 7 is good for many kinds of food crops.

Eve's Garden

When I first spoke with Eve about her garden, she told me she'd had little luck growing vegetables on her own. I met her at her home in the Santa Monica Mountains, which had mature pine trees, strawberry trees, native grasses, and jasmine and citrus trees well established in the landscape. She led me to the backyard and showed me the terraced area just in front of the citrus trees, where she had been growing vegetables. I saw that the rest of her landscaping was lush and thriving, but this area was bare except for a few struggling pepper plants. I picked up some of the soil and found that it was quite rocky. When I squeezed a handful of it between my fingers, the soil stuck together in hard clumps. It was heavy with clay. It was also irrigated improperly, as vegetables have different water requirements than the trees and ornamentals in the landscape. We had work to do.

I let Eve know that the soil needed to be amended and that it could take several years of adding in good amendments and compost before the soil really started to be healthy enough to produce the vegetables she was hoping for. I also adjusted the irrigation by removing the sprinkler heads in that area, putting in a new valve, and placing drip lines on their own timer so that the water requirements of the vegetables would be met. Next, I brought in organic compost and worked that into the soil using the double dig method, removing rocks and other debris as I did so.

Opposite
These gorgeous onions are a Mediterranean variety called Red Long of Tropea.

That next year produced higher yields of the tomatoes, peppers, and eggplant Eve likes to grow. But the yield wasn't anywhere near where it could be. Nature can be helped, but it can't really be rushed beyond a certain point. The following season we amended with more nitrogen-rich compost and alfalfa meal, plus rock phosphate for phosphorus and greensand, which is loaded with potassium. We amended the soil after each season, and by the third year the garden was booming with the foods that Eve and her family love to eat! Each year, Eve's garden grows healthier and more productive as the soil gets richer and full of these vital nutrients. We grew good soil, and it took time. Healthy soil can't be made overnight, but the fact is that it *can* be made as the seasons progress. You can turn a sand dune into a garden, and you can also reform a slick slab of clay. Now her garden is bountiful with perennials such as blueberries, asparagus, lemon verbena, and pomegranates as well as annuals such as tomatoes, peppers, garlic, kale, onions, fava beans, and spinach. If we continue to tend it well, the soil will accrue more and more organic matter and her harvests will continue to increase.

Garden Notes

1. Organic gardening is about growing and building healthy soil.
2. Compost is the key to healthy soil, no matter what your soil type.
3. Compost is easy to make from green and brown household materials.
4. Fertilizers are rated for nitrogen (N), phosphorous (P), and potassium (K).
5. Poor plant growth could indicate that soil pH is out of balance or minerals such as calcium, iron, and zinc are needed. Crop rotation is necessary to keep your soil from being depleted.

Opposite
Harvesting beans in Eve's garden. Beans are good nitrogen fixers and feed the soil as they feed us.

Above
Besides being sweet and delicious, peas also restore nitrogen to depleted beds.

CHAPTER FOUR

A Question of Water

I THINK ABOUT WATER and instinctually my eyes go to the plants outside my window. There are scores of potted plants outside the door here in our Laurel Canyon home: some smallish pots of herbs, raised beds of vegetables, and giant fruit trees in hulking wood planters that take four people to move. There's a mini-orchard out there, with figs, apples, plums, peaches, pomegranates, blood oranges, limes, lemons, and more. The hillside below was, unfortunately, terraced with treated railroad ties long before we arrived, so we couldn't put a garden in the ground. But growing in containers, without using drips on a timer, means paying special attention to water, and I scan the leaves and then the sky beyond. On this extremely hot day, the leaves are droopy. The plants need water. The steady and toasty breeze means the water is evaporating faster than normal. I drop what I'm doing and go outside to get some water in the soil.

Gardens are won and lost because of water. Not enough water or too much water both harm the soil and the crops. When I teach gardening workshops, one of the first questions I am usually asked is "How do I know how much water to give my garden?" We know intuitively that the way we water is as important as the way we prepare the soil, source the seeds, or pull the weeds. When we do this, we're stepping in to help the plants adjust to the water that is naturally available in the ground and brought by the weather.

Have you ever noticed that human beings all over the planet obsess about the weather? It doesn't matter if you're on the Mongolian steppe or in a Manhattan office tower or on a Michigan farm— people want to know if the skies are bringing sun or snow. That is partly because we worry about what to wear and whether we will be comfortable, but I believe it is mostly because we recognize that weather is bigger than all of us, completely out of our control and vital for the production of our food. Like our response to the soil, which calls out to us with information about its fertility or infertility, the trees and grass and dragon-tongue beans telegraph their thirst. When the earth is thirsty, we begin to crave a good rain or snow. As I write this, the Sierras in California are shaking off one of the biggest snowpacks in recent memory, and the swollen rivers are blasting through the canyons, picking up boulders the size of my truck. We've had a season of relief after years of crippling drought, and all winter we saw the trees put on new deep-green leaves. And yet by September, many of the feeder creeks in the mountains will be dry. California could return to drought. There is too much water, and then there is none again.

The drought brings the vital importance of having enough water to our doorstep. Chronic lack of water forced some Southern California farmers who are our friends to make extreme and difficult choices— some abandoned acres and acres of citrus trees to die off in order to reserve the water they had to save the pomegranates, which need less water and have a better chance of survival. Others saw animals who were driven by hunger out of the Sierras come down and destroy their entire crop.

So I feel a kinship with everyone on the planet; here we all are, up early like a bunch of farmers, checking our phones or huddling around crackly radios or watching the morning TV newscast, wondering, *What's the weather going to be like today?* I can't help believing that it's our dependence on water that makes us want to know.

Water is the most transient element in the garden. Other nutrients and elements can be depleted and replenished, but water goes the quickest and requires our regular attention. As Mary Oliver wrote, "Sometimes the river murmurs, sometimes it raves." The point is, the river talks, and we need to listen. Our job is to keep the garden at just the right amount of moist. We can't control the weather, but we can control the quantity of water we put on the garden. And because we're gardening organically, the humus in the soil drastically cuts down on the amount of water we use, sometimes by as much as 75 percent. We become the weather.

Opposite
Scarlet Flame Passion flower vines draw hummingbirds and butterflies to the garden and are not heavy water users. I like to grow these flowering vines on fences.

Above
When the season nears its end
and the plants bolt, broccoli and
arugula produce gorgeous flowers.
Broccoli flowers are edible and
have a sweet, nutty taste.

Opposite
Water is the most transient
element in the garden.

The Touch Test

One of the most accurate ways of finding out if your garden needs water is to put your finger in the soil. All farmers and gardeners do this, because it works. Poke your finger straight into the dirt and feel the soil 1 to 2 inches (2.5 to 5 cm) beneath the surface. If the soil is consistently moist down 2 inches (5 cm) and even beyond, then the soil has enough water. If it is dry, or there are spots of dry and wet, then the soil needs water. If it is soggy and mucky, then it has had too much water. Simple as that. If it is too wet, wait another day and check again.

Also, as I did at the beginning of this chapter, look at the plants: Are the leaves droopy? A tiny bit of droop is normal for a hot day—that's just the plant conserving water in the heat—but if the plants are really sagging, they need more water. Sometimes plants such as young broccoli get heat-stressed and literally flop right down on the dirt; they will likely recover with some water and cooler temps, but not without a little damage. Sometimes such plants will grow crooked or develop other weaknesses. We should never let the water in the soil get that low.

Opposite Left
One of the most accurate ways of finding out if your garden needs water is to put your finger in the soil.

Opposite Right
The leaves on these kumquat and tangerine trees are rolled and dry, telling us they may need more water.

Above Left
Citrus trees grow best in plant hardiness zones 8 to 11.

Above Right
When citrus is planted directly in the ground, the trees actually require less water as they mature.

How to Water

Yes, there's a technique to hand-watering, and it's easy to remember: First, you want to make it as gentle as rain; second, you're watering the soil, not the plants.

To make the watering gentle, I use a watering can or a watering wand that turns the water coming out of the hose into a sprinkler. You can also do this by placing your thumb over the end of the hose, if you're careful. This lets the water aerate on its way down and it doesn't hit the ground so hard. Firing water straight out of a hose in a jet compacts the soil and can hurt the plants.

It's not a bad thing to spray water on the leaves as long as they have time to dry out before nightfall; it can remove dust and make them more efficient at exchanging gases. But remember that it's not the plant that needs to get wet—it's the soil. Water enters the plants through the roots in the soil, so it's the soil that needs to be properly watered. The best plan is to direct the water at the soil at the base of the plant. Apply until there is standing water on the surface, and then pull the water away. If it seeps into the ground and is gone in one second, then give it some more. The water should stand on top of the ground for a few seconds before you move on.

Water Deeply

It is important to water the soil deeply so that the moisture goes several inches below the surface. If we water only the surface, the plants will develop shallow roots and will not grow and produce as they should. We need to water deeply so plants can develop profound and healthy roots. A good foundation brings rewards.

Sometimes soil can look bone-dry on top, but feeling below the surface can turn up moist soil. The opposite might occur as well. One of the most common mistakes in watering gardens is that we water only the top layer and move the hose away before enough moisture seeps down into the deeper layers of soil, where mature plant roots are located. If we go back and put a finger in the watered soil, we may find that it is dry below the surface and we did not give enough water to the soil.

In the unrelenting heat of summer, some gardens need to be watered twice a day, preferably in the early morning and then late in the afternoon, after the heat of the day has passed. I try not to water gardens in the evening and especially not at night— water can cling to leaves after sunset, when the air turns cooler. Leaves left wet overnight invite powdery mildew that hurts the plants, especially beans, squash, and cucumbers.

Opposite
A good watering can helps ensure that water is distributed evenly and gently throughout the garden.

Above
A vegetable garden housed within a drought-tolerant landscape

Above Left
Morning dew on the pea vines

Above Right
Broccoli leaves still wet from the rain

Opposite
Both Genovese and opal basil can grow beautifully in an arid canyon, because drip irrigation lines run through the raised beds to deliver just the right amount of water. The flowers are delicious to use in the kitchen, and harvesting them regularly keeps basil plants healthy.

Throwing Some Shade

Plants need to grow in full sun, but the exposed soil between the plants doesn't benefit as much from all this heat. The sun sucks the water right out of the soil. In some very extreme climates, such as Arizona in the dead of summer, gardens can benefit from shade netting, which is stretched over the plants to give them a little break from the sun. But we can also help shade the earth between the plants by growing them close together. Most types of plants really don't mind this at all, and you get more food out of a smaller area while at the same time the soil stays moist. This might make weeding slightly more challenging, but the trade-offs in less water usage and more food are worth it.

Left
Shade makes this garden lush.
Growing plants and trees with
similar watering needs together
helps ensure that the garden
will thrive.

Irrigation Methods

The alternative to watering by hand is to put in a simple irrigation system of drip lines and a timer. Using a drip irrigation system on a timer ensures that the garden receives regular, deep watering even if you are travelling or away from home. These systems also deliver water right to the soil and avoid getting the leaves wet, which means you can water later in the evening and earlier in the morning.

If you decide to put in an irrigation system, I recommend installing drip lines made from tubing with an outside diameter of 1/4 inch (6 mm) along the length of the garden, spaced 6 inches (15 cm) apart. The tubes in a small garden connect to one main header tube, usually 1/2 inch (1.2 cm), so they can all be run with one water valve and timer. (See the accompanying photos for how we normally set this up.) Your lawn sprinklers might already have valves and timers, but vegetable garden irrigation should have its own valve and timer. The water needs of the vegetable garden are different from the requirements of the grass, trees, and other plants in

the landscape, therefore, they need their own valve to control the amount of water they receive. You can put the vegetables on their own station on your current timer, or put them on their own, separate timer. The advantage of putting the vegetable garden on its own timer is that you can keep its water on at times when the timer that controls other areas of the garden is turned off due to rains or other issues.

You will need to experiment a little with your drip lines to figure out how long they need to run and on how many days per week. If you live in a wet or humid climate and get a decent amount of summer rainfall, they might not need to run very often. When it's hot and dry, they will need to run more frequently. Remember that hot and humid days *feel* more critical, because the humidity makes us sweat, but actually a dry wind will cause much more water to evaporate. Your watering schedule will need to be adjusted in different seasons and as the weather shifts. Here, in Southern California, we start by setting the drips to go off three times a week for eighteen minutes and then fine tune it from there. The climate on the East Coast is more humid, in general, so gardens there might need less water. The number of minutes depends on the water pressure, too. The higher the pressure, the less time the drips should run.

Opposite
A drip irrigation system on a timer gives the soil regular, deep watering even if you are travelling or away from your garden.

Above
The ¼ inch (6 mm) drip lines in this raised garden bed all run into one main header irrigation line, usually ½-inch (1.2-cm) plastic tubing.

There are some easy ways to judge whether the drip lines are working right. First, check the soil with your finger test. Also, if you see water coming out from the bottom of raised beds, you know you have too many minutes and/or days on the timer. If you have an in-ground garden and the soil is too wet, you need to dial it back to fewer days or shorter runs per day. Figuring out the right amount of water for the garden is not difficult at all, but it requires our attention, just like watching the weather

Garden Notes

1. Both underwatering and overwatering will hurt the garden.
2. Test the soil by sticking a finger in it.
3. Water deeply: Puddles should sit on the surface for a couple of seconds before disappearing.
4. Grow plants closer together to shade the soil
5. Use drip-line irrigation for more precise and regular watering.

Above
Drip lines can be placed between the poles of a trellis to ensure even irrigation throughout the entire garden bed.

Opposite
Popcorn cassia is an ornamental shrub whose yellow flowers smell like buttered popcorn. This shrub attracts bees and butterflies to the garden and likes wet, tropical conditions.

Growing in New England
Beth Schiller of Dandelion Spring Farm

Below
Beth Schiller of Dandelion Spring Farm with her hogs

Opposite
"Food grown locally and picked fresh and eaten while it's fresh feels different in our bodies."
—Beth Schiller

We are richer for the relationships we form around food. Here, and on page 220, we have profiled two farms we admire and who have taught us so much. These are farmers who grow in different ways, but what they share is their commitment to feeding their communities.

I first met Beth Schiller at the farmers market in Deering Oaks Park in Portland, Maine, around 2010, and for years I have enjoyed the gorgeous organic food she grows at her Dandelion Spring Farm. I have lived a lot of my life in Maine, and she is everything I like about the people there: no-nonsense, practical, funny, resilient, so smart, and so connected to the land and to the seasons. She knows the whole farm and at various times has offered a full-diet CSA (Community-Supported Agriculture) package, which means she provides vegetables, meat, herbs, milk, eggs—everything. I carry her herbal tinctures and soaps in my Edible Gardens LA online shop, and I feel so lucky to be able to share farm questions with her.

My initial experience in gardens was in New England, and growing plants there is very different, of course, than in Southern California, where I live now. But as Beth and I walked and talked on her farm, it became clear the difference is mostly a matter of dates: In Maine, where winters can be severe, you may start your vegetables like peppers or eggplant in a hothouse or in your kitchen window in the first week of March, but you have to wait until after the last frost before putting them in the ground. Beth's farm is in Plant Hardiness Zone 5a, which means the last frost in the spring is around May 15. However, in Midcoast Maine in recent years, they've had frost as late as June, and are prepared for it coming back again in the beginning of September.

Farmers are sensitive to those dates, but are constantly working to push the season. Beth can't afford to be constrained so she's now growing year-round, and more and more farmers and home gardeners are doing the same.

A GARDEN CAN BE ANYWHERE

"More and more, it's three hundred sixty-five here," says Beth. "When I started farming in 1998, the goal was to make enough money in the summer to not have to farm in the winter. But now, there are a lot of small organic farms. The organic farming network, Maine Organic Farming and Gardening Association, is really strong, so it's drawn a lot of new farms. The competition is getting pretty steep. Part of that balance is to have your crop year-round. We fill these greenhouses with cold-hardy greens. It can be minus-two Fahrenheit [–19 C] and these little lettuce heads make it. It's amazing. And arugula. And scallions. We have those year-round.

"We balance it by stockpiling walk-in coolers with carrots, beets, turnips, potatoes, and other roots. Now our farmers market and our whole-sale accounts go year-round. And the meats help. As a market gardener, that's the goal. But also for the home gardener; there's more and more education from people like Elliot Coleman about how you can locally produce healthy food year-round."

As we walk through Beth's hothouses, we see that some of them are for starting crops in trays and others allow planting directly in the ground.

"The seasons don't change. We still have winter. And yet we're pushing it with plastic [hothouses], and I think farmers are becoming more and more savvy about what varieties can take the cold. I grow this little Salanova lettuce that freezes; it gets down below zero, and it's hardy. It just keeps going. I don't heat those houses."

Lauri: Do you use cold frames?
Beth: No. I used to, but in terms of scale, cold frames don't provide a lot of interior space. I'd need many of them, and I'm worried about edge effect. Even this little twelve-foot-wide [3.5 meter] roundhouse—I have to be very selective of what is in there in the winter. It doesn't do nearly as well as what is in the wider, twenty-six-to thirty-foot [8–9 meter] houses. Whatever is on the edges is significantly more prone to cold

Opposite
Amaranth flowers on Beth's farm

Below
Dandelion Springs has grown whole-diet menus, which include meat and poultry.

Following Pages
Dandelion Spring Farm is a certified organic farm.

damage. Also, I'm in a climate where it can be below freezing for long stretches of time. Plants need a little more cushion to recover from that than if they were in a climate where it just occasionally got below freezing. In that instance, I might be less concerned about the effect of the edge of the house being colder.

Lauri: One of your goals is to pay attention to soil nutrition and to guard the soil. What do you mean by that?

Beth: Well, I eat vegetables because they're healthy for me. And all those nutrients came from the soil. So I want that soil to be at least as nutrient-rich, if not more nutrient-rich, than how it started before we took out the vegetables. Even just feeding a family off a small space, the soil can help us to produce hundreds of pounds of vegetables that are made up of nutrients and water. And those nutrients need to be returned to the ground in order for the soil to continue to feed you. I also think that it's important to not forget all the microorganisms and the environment that's under the soil, too.

As a production farmer, I think it's really easy to get into "I want more carrots." To get into the economics. But that's only half of it.

Lauri: How do we build a human community that is more garden- and farm-conscious? How did you get into it?

Beth: I grew up in Maine, west of here, and I always loved sheep and I was always interested in creating my own food and fiber. When I was in college, I learned that farming was a really excellent metaphor for talking about other environmental issues. I was at a liberal arts college that allowed me the freedom to go out to farms and talk about the things that were important to me in a way that was also very accessible. I was interested in the effects of the growth of urban areas on rural areas, and how that was impacting those rural communities economically, as well as socially. This was the mid-nineties, and people were starting to talk a little bit about climate change. Also realizing that our food is coming from farther away, and what is the environmental and economic impact of that?

Lauri: Does it help when people can see the farm?

Beth: One thing I have very consciously tried, especially in the last seven years, is to get the farmers market customers to the farm. Because there are people like you who see our farmstand, but it's a totally different emotional impact to see the carrots and beets in the ground, and hear the turkeys, and have the

Below
"When I was in college, I learned that farming was a really excellent metaphor for talking about other environmental issues."
—Beth Schiller

Opposite
Just-picked organic tomatoes for the Dandelion Spring Farm stand at the Portland Farmers Market

dog obsessively give you the stick. I want them to have that experience—both for them to get a better sense for where their food is coming from, and because it impacts that discussion of why farming and farmland are important.

I think that one of the more important conversations we need to be having in New England is how to make this food accessible to the population that isn't getting it. We live in what some people refer to as the "Gold Coast" part of Maine, that tends to be liberal and fairly affluent. But there is a huge percentage of people in Maine, and a huge percentage of farmers, who are part of the food stamp system, or EBT. So figuring out how to make that population aware of the local food, and how to support the farmers and to make that food affordable and accessible, that's the conversation that farmers are really trying to breach here.

Lauri: Part of that discussion is rediscovering the home garden.

Beth: For farms, the entry point is eggs. For some reason, people still know that a fresh farm egg is different from a grocery store egg. So that's the first drop-in. One of the connections is to realize that food grown locally and picked fresh and eaten while it's fresh feels different in our bodies. If I get people here, then they will eat the fresh carrot, or the fresh egg, and then consciously or unconsciously, they may recognize that they feel different in their body. Then that helps the next step, which is: Okay, how am I going to make this a priority? Which is good for their health. And it's good for the economy. And it's good for keeping the land open.

One thing that I find really valuable about books about how you grow food is that it's going to inspire someone else to grow their own food, and then they're going to get that reaction, or interaction. You know? And then that furthers the conversation, too.

Later, sitting around a picnic table under a tree, Beth pulls out her newest collection of herbal tinctures and infusions, which she makes from her own organic tulsi basil, lemon verbena, sorrel, hyssop, fennel, calendula, and other plants, and some wild-picked herbs, like colt's foot. Some of these are nonalcoholic infusions in delicious apple cider vinegar and honey, and others are alcoholic tinctures in 150-proof certified-organic vodka made by a local distillery that also feeds its grain waste to her cows! Like Beth, I consider medicinal herbs to be a gardener's art that has faded and can be so practical, like mullein oil for treating ear infections and oregano oil for a bad stomach, or hyssop for respiratory health and strength-enhancing ashwagandha.

A GARDEN CAN BE ANYWHERE

And some of the herbs are more mysterious, like tulsi, which shows that one of the bottom lines in farming is not just economics, but health. I pick up one bottle and regard it.

Lauri: I'm curious about tulsi. I don't understand it very well.

Beth: Tulsi, I think, is a magic plant. Tulsi is a very strong adaptogen; it can tell what your body needs. I grow it here. When I studied very briefly with an herbalist in India, she told me: If you have any plant in your garden, this is it. And I initially went to her because I was working a lot with the tulsi and I just loved it. As an adaptogen: It will help strengthen, it will help calm; it goes to what you need. It's hard to talk about it without sounding like a hippie woo-woo plant person, but tulsi is simply a very powerful plant.

Beth and I laughed about this. We focus so hard on making the most delicious tomato, or delivering to a chef the ideal purple bok choy. But maybe what your body needs is a few leaves of tulsi. Every day I discover more mystery and more beauty in the garden. What will you plant in yours?

Opposite
Dandelion Spring Farm's tinctures, elixirs, and oils are made on the farm, from ingredients grown and harvested on the farm. Like Beth, I consider medicinal herbs to be a gardener's art.

CHAPTER FIVE

Plant What You Love

(and One Thing You Don't)

DECIDING WHAT TO GROW and where to plant those first seeds and seedlings in a new vegetable garden is an exciting and especially creative time. Perennial trees such as apple, avocado, or lemon trees deliver fruit for many years, but in an annual vegetable garden each season is a clean slate, with newly amended garden beds just waiting to express your latest thinking. Perhaps you're planting corn seeds passed down from a grandparent, which makes yours an heirloom garden. Or maybe you want to experiment with three types of peppers. How do you arrange the plants in the garden? Will broccoli thrive next to cilantro? Do you have room for giant fava bean plants? What do you use the most in the kitchen? Your intuition will give you a lot of answers to questions like these, but a little planning can help your garden thrive.

We want both bounty and flavor from the garden. Some things we grow in small amounts because their strong flavors go a long way, such as habanero peppers and oregano. But other things we grow for volume. In the cool season, for instance, leafy greens such as kale, Swiss chard, lettuce, arugula, mustard greens, and spinach give us large amounts of food as we harvest them leaf by leaf, over and over again throughout the season. As we cut the leaves off these plants, they are quickly and constantly replenished; a relatively small number of Swiss chard plants can provide a family several meals per week for an entire season! Similarly, delicious Sungold tomatoes keep producing and producing over several months.

Other things come all at once: We wait for peas and then they come into harvest in heaps.

Most of us grow in smaller spaces, and we have to be mindful of how to make the best use of our garden. Cauliflower is a wonderful vegetable to grow, but it's helpful to know that it takes up a lot of room in the garden as we wait to harvest it. Multi-headed broccoli, on the other hand, takes up just about the same amount of space and is a big producer, filling our harvest baskets week after week, and can be a better choice if space is limited.

What we grow is also sometimes a matter of our market and cooking habits. Some of us want to grow all our own tomatoes or all our own greens, but then buy the rest of what we need at the market. Others want to grow a little bit of everything and augment as needed. It's hard to limit ourselves when there is so much promise in each new seed!

Opposite
Bee balm attracts bees and butterflies and makes beautiful cut flowers.

Below
Lettuce is space-efficient and gives us large amounts of food as we harvest it leaf by leaf, over and over again throughout the season.

Cooking from the Garden

Gardening has changed the way I cook. When we're used to having a recipe in front of us as we cook, growing a little bit of everything can present challenges at mealtime: We come in from the garden clutching six leaves of Swiss chard, a handful of kale, and a head of broccoli. What can you make with that? It can be hard to find a recipe that uses these bits and parts, as most recipes feature one veggie or another as the main ingredient or call for specific amounts of ingredients that you might not have available. However, gardens have helped me to let go in the kitchen. Now I grow what I love and let the harvest basket dictate what's for dinner. In Italy, it has long been the way to plan a meal: You just go into the garden and cook whatever it gives you. In France, "ratatouille" literally means "a motley stew"! Though traditionally made with tomatoes and eggplant, it can be made with anything from the garden, all put together into a delicious meal.

I have found that I can do a lot with the small bits of leafy greens and broccoli coming out of the garden. I like to stir-fry it all together with garlic, olive oil, and cooked brown rice, slice an avocado on top, and finish it off with freshly squeezed lemon juice, good olive oil, and salt. I also enjoy taking that same odds-and-ends harvest of Swiss chard, kale, and broccoli and using it to top homemade pizza dough before popping it in the oven. The garden has made me a better and more creative cook than I ever was before. When our food is this fresh, it can only be delicious!

Above
Growing peas, cauliflower, beets, and more in the cool season garden

Opposite
The end-of-the-season broccoli harvest is still delicious with its sweet, nutty flowers.

Approximate range of average annual minumum temperatures for each zone.

2	Below -50°
3	-50° to -40°
4	-40° to -30°
5	-30° to -20°
6	-20° to -10°
7	0° to 10°
8	10° to 20°
9	20° to 30°
10	30° to 40°

What to Plant and When to Plant It

To help clients narrow the choice of vegetables to grow, I often give them a seasonal planting list based on where their garden is located and ask them to choose what they would like to grow from that list. From there, we work through their list to figure out what will grow best in the garden that they have, taking into consideration both the size of their plot and what they want to eat at harvest time.

Because we can amend the soil to address any deficiencies, the climate determines which vegetables grow best in your area. It's all about the weather!

Climates in the United States have been assigned zone numbers in order to help us decide what to plant; if you live in Cambridge, Massachusetts, for example, you live in zone 6b. You can use the easy-to-find online USDA Plant Hardiness Zone Map to figure out which zone you live in; just enter your zip code to learn your growing zone. When you find your zone, pay attention to the average last frost and first frost dates. Those help us determine when to put our seeds and seedling transplants into the ground.

Seed packages usually provide instructions for planting based on your last frost and first frost dates, and whether you should start the seeds indoors or outdoors. For example, if you are growing beans, the seed pack will tell you to sow the seeds

outdoors one to two weeks after the average last frost. If you want to grow cucumbers, the seed pack will tell you to start seeds *indoors* a couple of weeks before the last frost and then transplant them outside one to two weeks after the last frost, when soil temperatures reach 70°F (21°C). Depending on your zone, you may start tomatoes indoors six to eight weeks before the last frost. The zone you live in tells you the growing plan that works best for your garden.

But wait: Start seedlings *indoors*? Where do you do that? I start my plants by seeding them in a pot or in individual seedling trays, and then I simply set them in a sunny window. Remember how you did it in school, starting radishes in a half-gallon milk carton with the top cut off? It still works great. You may end up with a lot of plants taking up window-sills in the house—look out if you have a cat—but they sprout and grow just fine. Sometimes the simplest ways are best.

If the seedlings need to be outdoors, try a cold frame, which is generally a wood box with a glass lid and filled with soil. The heat of the sun keeps the plants growing inside even when there is snow outside. There are also lots of types of "quick hoops" available, which are like plastic tents that sit on top of your outdoor garden and warm the soil. Both work great. But don't worry about making anything too fancy!

Above
Greenhouses at Chase Farm in Maine allow for cultivation in cold weather.

Opposite
Use the USDA Plant Hardiness Zone Map available online to get detailed information about the growing zone you live in.

A GARDEN CAN BE ANYWHERE

Starting from Starts

Some plants are simply easier to grow as seedlings before transplanting to the garden, even if you're not starting them indoors or while there's still snow on the ground or for other climate reasons. These seedlings are often called "starts." Again, you're doing this in planting trays or small pots.

I find the following vegetables have a higher rate of germination and a better chance at survival if you plant them as starts:

Broccoli

Brussels sprouts

Cabbage

Cauliflower

Collards

Eggplant

Kale

Lettuce

Okra

Peppers

Shallots

Spinach

Swiss chard

Tomatoes

These do better if you sow them directly into the soil as seeds:

Beets

Carrots

Corn

Cucumbers

Fennel

Jerusalem artichokes
    (sunchokes)

Melons

Peas

Potatoes

Pumpkins

Radishes

Rutabagas

Squash

Turnips

Watermelons

Opposite
Kale seedlings in the foreground, ready to be transplanted into the garden beds

Below Left
Peppers can be started indoors or in a hoophouse during cold weather and then transplanted when the soil temperature rises outdoors.

Below Right
Squash blossoms in the warm season garden, a chef favorite. Harvest these when the flowers open in the early morning hours. The flowers close as the day warms up.

Below
Tap the bottom of the plastic
container to remove the spinach
seedlings. Keep the entire root ball
intact.

Opposite
Cover the roots entirely. Seedlings
can be transplanted outdoors when
they have three or four of their true
leaves, and the soil temperature
outdoors has warmed.

When to Transplant?

Seedlings can be transplanted outdoors when they
have three or four of their true leaves, and the soil
temperature outdoors has warmed. True leaves are
the leaves that grow after the cotyledons, which are
the first couple of leaves that appear on the seedling
after it has pushed out of the earth. If you still have
several weeks to go before the outdoor soil temp
will be high enough, you will want to pull up the
tiny seedlings and transplant them into larger pots
to keep them healthy as they grow.

When transplanting, take all the dirt and roots with
the plant if you can. If you start them in individual
seedling trays, empty each individual cube by tilt-
ing the seedling tray to the side and squeezing the
plant out from the bottom. Try not to pull a seedling
straight out of the tray, as the stem can break off
from the roots, killing the tender seedling. Put the
seedling with the soil it has grown in into the new
spot and water well.

Warm and Cool Season Vegetables

Garden fruits and vegetables can be broken down into warm season and cool season crops. The cool season vegetables are ideally grown when soil temperatures range between 50 and 70°F (10 and 21°C). Warm season crops are best grown when soil temperatures reach 70°F (21°C) and above. As mentioned earlier, seed packets will let you know which seeds need to be started indoors and then transplanted outside once soil temperatures have warmed.

Above Left
Asparagus, a cool-season plant, ready for harvest

Above Right
Carrots freshly pulled during the cool season

Opposite Left
Haricots verts, or French green beans, in the warm season garden

Opposite Right
Warm-season eggplant comes in many delicious varieties, including Dancer, Beatrice, and Black Beauty.

WHAT TO GROW AND
WHEN TO GROW IT

Cool Season

Artichokes
Asparagus
Beets
Broccoli
Brussels sprouts
Cabbage
Carrots
Cauliflower
Celery
Chicory

Chinese cabbage
Collards
Fava beans
Fennel
Garlic
Kale
Kohlrabi
Leeks
Lettuce
Mustard greens
Onions

Parsnips
Peas
Potatoes
Radishes
Rutabagas
Shallots
Spinach
Swiss chard
Turnips

Warm Season

Beans
Corn
Cucumbers
Eggplant
Melons
Okra
Peppers
Pumpkins
Squash
Tomatillos
Tomatoes
Watermelon

How to Plant from Seed

When starting vegetables from seed, take a look at the seed you are planting. A good rule of thumb is that the bigger the seed, the deeper it will go into the soil. Small seeds need to be closer to the surface. Larger seeds need a little more soil cover. Almost every seed packet will give you seed depth recommendations. The tiniest seeds only need to be pressed into the surface of the soil; slightly bigger seeds such as broccoli and kale go in ¼ inch (6 mm); and fava beans need to go 1 inch (2.5 cm) deep, or to the end of the first knuckle on your pointer finger. Potatoes are one of the deepest and need 3 inches (7.5 cm) of soil on top. Once they are in the soil, water immediately.

Placing and Spacing
Each seed also needs to be correctly spaced from its neighbor, and those spacings are usually marked on the seed packaging, too. Tomatoes need to be 3 to 4 feet (.9 to 1.2 m) apart, but radishes can be as close as ½ inch (1.3 cm) from one another. It's worth the time to plant them carefully.

I don't generally plant in rows, as I like a more wild garden style, so I simply eyeball the spacing of one plant to the next. Rows can be good, however, if you decide to plant a more extensive in-ground garden. For one, rows give you a place to stand to do your weeding and harvesting without crushing the plants or compacting the soil. And two, planting in rows can allow you to use a precision seeder, which is a garden hand-tool that drops seeds in a furrow at regular preset intervals while you pull it through the garden. A seeder can give you perfect rows, and perfectly spaced plants, and costs between one hundred and two hundred dollars. For the kind of gardening I do, though, it's not necessary.

Above and Below
Sowing flower seeds next to the vegetable seedlings brings diversity, beauty, and beneficial pollinators to the garden.

Opposite
When starting vegetables from seed, a good rule of thumb is that the bigger the seed, the deeper it will go into the soil. Small seeds need to be closer to the surface. Larger seeds need a little more soil cover.

A GARDEN CAN BE ANYWHERE

How to Plant from Seedlings

If you're buying seedlings from a trusted grower or nursery, look for the ones that appear healthiest, with straight, robust stems. Choose less mature seedlings that are not yet flowering or producing tiny peppers, tomatoes etc. Seedlings need water daily and when they don't get it, they sometimes flop right down on the dirt; they recover easily, but sometimes the stems are permanently damaged and the plant will grow bent. Make sure there aren't too many yellow or dead leaves. A few bug-munched leaves won't matter, but just make sure there are no live pests on the plant, such as aphids.

The seedlings will most likely be in seedling trays or small pots. Tap the tray or pot to loosen the dirt and tiny roots from the plastic, then take the whole root ball and all the dirt with it, and place it in the ground. Dig your hole to a depth so the top of the base of the stem comes out about level with the garden soil. I usually give the seedlings a dose of liquid seaweed and then some water to help them survive the shock of transplantation.

Opposite
Healthy eggplant seedlings ready to transplant into the vegetable beds. If you're buying seedlings from a trusted grower or nursery, look for the ones that appear healthiest, with straight, robust stems.

Above Left
Dig your hole to a depth so the top of the root ball is about level with the garden soil.

Above Right
Cover the roots of the newly transplanted seedlings with plenty of good soil.

Right
Transplanting eggplant seedlings
into the vegetable beds

Trellises and Other Supports

When planning your garden, keep in mind that certain vegetables will need a trellis for support. Bush beans grow on self-standing plants, but runner and climbing beans need a trellis. Tomatoes need support to help keep their stalks, stems, and leaves upright and their heavy fruits from hitting the soil as they grow over the season. Peas come in both bush and climbing varieties for shelling and snap alike. Climbing varieties will need the aid of a trellis as they reach up toward the sun. I don't use supports for fava beans; instead I like to plant their seeds close together and allow them to lean on one another. As a rule, I grow cucumbers on a trellis; however, they are also good producers if left to wander on the soil or spill over the sides of a raised garden bed. Smaller melons and winter squash are happy to climb up fences and trellises or even up and over a pergola.

There are many options for trellising plants. My favorite is a bamboo teepee, which can be purchased already assembled or easily built at home with supplies from your local nursery or hardware store. It is freestanding and sturdy, and plants can climb it from outside and inside.

Another easy type of trellis to build involves pounding two posts of untreated wood into the ground, connecting the posts with a crossbar or a wire, and then stringing twine vertically from the crossbar or wire to a stake in the ground next to each plant. Tomatoes and cucumbers love to climb that twine. Another option is to make a loose mesh from that twine and hang it from the crossbar, as peas love to climb a mesh.

A segment of lattice fencing can also make a great trellis. Many people grow vegetables on their garden fence or on a gate or archway that leads to the garden, which can make for a beautiful invitation to interact with what's planted there. Just remember that whatever you grow on the outermost fence of your property might be vulnerable to deer and other visitors, so you may need a more secure fence around your whole property in order to make that work.

Opposite Top Left
Pea seeds ready for planting

Opposite Top Right
Plant climbing peas around the base of a trellis.

Opposite Bottom Left
Cover freshly planted seeds with soil.

Opposite Bottom Right
Sugar snap peas ready for picking

Companion Planting

Plants have friends, too! There are plants that do best in the garden when surrounded by other plants that we call companion plants, meaning that one helps the other grow. There are also plants that can hinder the health and growth of other plants, so it's good to identify these and keep them apart. The more you grow, the more you discover what works best in your own garden. Below is a companion planting chart to help you get started.

Companion Planting

BEANS
Companions: beets (only to bush beans), cabbage, broccoli, cauliflower, Brussels sprouts, kohlrabi, collards, kale, carrots, celery, chard, corn, cucumbers, eggplant, peas, potatoes, radishes, strawberries
Foes: garlic, onions, shallots

BEETS
Companions: bush beans, cabbage, broccoli, cauliflower, Brussels sprouts, kohlrabi, collards, kale, lettuce, onions
Foe: pole beans

BROCCOLI
Companions: beets, celery, chard, cucumbers, lettuce, onions, potatoes, spinach

BRUSSELS SPROUTS
Companions: beets, celery, chard, cucumbers, lettuce, onions, potatoes, spinach

CABBAGE
Companions: beets, celery, chard, cucumbers, lettuce, onions, potatoes, spinach

CARROTS
Companions: beans, chamomile, garlic, lettuce, onions, peas, peppers, radishes, tomatoes
Foe: dill

CAULIFLOWER
Companions: beets, celery, chard, cucumbers, lettuce, onions, potatoes, spinach

CELERY
Companions: beans, cabbage, broccoli, cauliflower, Brussels sprouts, kohlrabi, collards, kale, tomatoes

CHARD
Companions: beans, cabbage, broccoli, cauliflower, Brussels sprouts, kohlrabi, collards, kale, onions

CORN
Companions: beans, cucumbers, melons, parsley, peas, potatoes, pumpkins, squash
Foe: tomatoes

CUCUMBERS
Companions: beans, cabbage, broccoli, cauliflower, Brussels sprouts, kohlrabi, collards, kale, corn, peas, radishes, tomatoes
Foe: sage

EGGPLANT
Companions: beans, peppers

KALE
Companions: beets, celery, chard, cucumbers, lettuce, onions, potatoes, spinach

KOHLRABI

Companions: beets, celery, chard, cucumbers, lettuce, onions, potatoes, spinach

LETTUCE

Companions: beets, cabbage, broccoli, cauliflower, Brussels sprouts, kohlrabi, collards, kale, carrots, onions, radishes, strawberries

MELONS

Companions: corn, pumpkins, radishes, squash

ONIONS

Companions: beets, cabbage, broccoli, cauliflower, Brussels sprouts, kohlrabi, collards, kale, carrots, chard, lettuce, peppers, strawberries, tomatoes
Foes: beans, peas

PEAS

Companions: beans, carrots, corn, cucumbers, radishes, turnips
Foes: garlic, onions

PEPPERS

Companions: carrots, eggplant, onions, tomatoes

POTATOES

Companions: beans, cabbage, broccoli, cauliflower, Brussels sprouts, kohlrabi, collards, kale, corn, eggplant, peas
Foe: tomatoes

PUMPKINS

Companions: corn, melons, squash

RADISHES

Companions: beans, carrots, cucumbers, lettuce, melons, peas
Foe: hyssop

SPINACH

Companions: cabbage, broccoli, cauliflower, Brussels sprouts, kohlrabi, collards, kale, strawberries

SQUASH

Companions: beans, borage, corn, melons, pumpkins,

STRAWBERRIES

Companions: beans, lettuce, onions, spinach, thyme

TOMATOES

Companions: asparagus, borage, basil, carrots, celery, cucumbers, onions, parsley, peppers
Foes: corn, dill, kohlrabi, potatoes

TURNIPS

Companions: beans, cabbage, broccoli, cauliflower, Brussels sprouts, kohlrabi, collards, kale, corn, eggplant, peas

Opposite Left
Companion planting is an important part of a healthy garden. Broccoli and beets are good neighbors and help each other grow.

Opposite Right
Fava beans and cilantro flowers share the garden bed. The cilantro flowers will produce fresh green coriander seeds as these fava beans mature, making for delicious possibilities in the kitchen.

Above Left
Spicy peppers are abundant producers and easy to grow, and they love the company of Queen Anne's Lace.

Above Right
Poppies, broccoli, and carrots growing together

Herbs

One of the keys to great home cooking is to have fresh herbs growing within easy reach of the kitchen, and it's so simple to do. Mine are all in medium-size pots spread around a sunny deck just outside the kitchen door. If you're going to build a separate herb garden in the ground, or in a dedicated raised bed, do yourself a favor and place it close to the house. That makes it simple to dash out the door when you have a pot on the stove to snip some basil or rosemary as needed. It's a great job for the kids when you're all in the kitchen together!

Be sure to grow the basics that you use regularly in your cooking. I always need rosemary, basil, parsley, dill, cilantro, sage, and thyme. When you plant rosemary, give it a spot where it has room to grow and it will take over! Trim it back regularly; if you don't, in a year or three it will be a bush as big as your car.

Other standards are oregano, lemon verbena, marjoram, tarragon, chives, chervil, and mint. These are all readily available as seedlings or seeds. Mint needs to be planted in its own pot, as it is invasive and will quickly take over the garden.

Many herbs are perennials, such as rosemary and lemon verbena, so you just harvest when you need it. If you live in a colder climate, growing herbs in a cold frame or a quick hoop will allow you and your family to enjoy fresh herbs for much of the year.

Left
Anise Hyssop is a beautiful addition to the vegetable beds. It makes tall purple flowers as the plant matures. The leaves have a light licorice-minty taste and make a wonderful tea that helps to soothe the stomach.

Opposite
Italian basil flowers need to be snipped off to encourage healthy leaf growth and keep the plant producing

Pages 174–175
Amaranth flowers come in many beautiful varieties.

The World Needs Flowers *(and So Does Your Vegetable Garden)*

Flowers are vital for a healthy, well-balanced garden. Flowers bring the bees and butterflies and create a beautiful place for all kinds of creatures to nourish and nurture the garden. I interplant them all through the gardens. They add beauty and good health to the garden soil. I have favorite flowers for the vegetable beds.

HERE ARE A FEW:

Amaranth
Anemone
Bachelor Button
Bee balm
Bells of Ireland
Borage
Carrot flower
Cosmo
Dahlia (dinnerplate variety)
Eryngium
French marigold
Larkspur

Lupine
Nasturtium
Nigella
Poppy
Queen Anne's lace
Salvia
Scabiosa
Stock
Sunflower
Sweet pea
Sweet William
Verbena
Wildflowers
Yarrow

Above Left
Fennel flowers bring pollinators and are wonderful host plants for caterpillars and butterflies of many varieties.

Above Right
Wild carrot flowers are one of my favorites.

Opposite
Poppy flowers add a pop of color and beauty to the garden.

There are also herbs and certain vegetables that I like to let go to seed just for their flowers!

HERE ARE SOME OF THOSE:

Arugula
Bergamot
Calendula
Chamomile
Chives

Comfrey
Fennel
Oregano
Valerian

Crop Rotation

We rotate the location of plants in the garden so that both soil and plants stay healthy season after season. Plants from the same vegetable families need to be rotated throughout the garden to help prevent soil disease and to replenish the soil. I rotate plants that are heavy nitrogen users with those that give nitrogen to the soil (see Chapter Three). For example, after tomatoes (heavy feeders) have been pulled, grow fava beans or peas. After carrots, grow beans. There is a rhythm that you will develop with your own garden that will give you a natural, or organic, way of mapping out your plantings each new season.

Below
After this harvest of tatsoi, kale, and broccoli, I plant beans and peas to restore nitrogen to the soil.

Crop Succession

Crop rotation means moving crops season to season, so that all the summertime crops (for example) change their positions from one year to the next. During a single season, however, it is often the case that one crop is finished before the others. For instance, you might cut arugula for a month and then it flowers and is done, but it's too early to rotate all your crops. Instead of leaving that space empty, you can plant a second crop for the season in that same space; the key is to change the crop. Don't plant more arugula. Instead, plant something else relatively fast-growing, such as radishes.

Below
Scarlet runner bean flowers are a dazzling addition to the garden, and are a great follow-up to corn or tomatoes.

Opposite
Try growing tomatillos to use in
salsas and sauces.

One Thing You Don't

After choosing all your favorite vegetables to plant
in a given season, take another look and pick something to grow that you don't usually eat. Perhaps
kohlrabi or sunchokes. This is part of the adventure,
and who knows what kind of dining experience
could result?

For instance, I never gravitated much toward
eating cabbage. It seemed the opposite of exotic:
I ate very bland stuffed cabbage growing up and I
thought of cabbage as mushy and uninteresting.
When I began growing my own food, I ended up
with some cabbage seedlings and planted them in
the garden. As they came into harvest, I wasn't sure
what to do with them so I just chopped them up and
sautéed them with olive oil, garlic, and salt. It was
absolutely delicious! A whole new world of cabbage
opened up to me. Now I grow it every season and use
it as a staple in our meals.

Garden Notes

1. Know your Plant Hardiness Zone.
2. Seed packets generally tell you when to plant
   according to first frost dates. Some will need
   to start indoors.
3. Some plants start better from seeds, and
   some from seedlings.
4. There are warm season plants and cool
   season plants.
5. The bigger the seed, the deeper they go into
   the soil.
6. Plant spacing matters, but they don't have to
   be in rows.
7. Some plants will need supports such as
   trellises or cages.
8. Companions plants help each other grow,
   and foes don't.
9. Grow herbs close to the kitchen.
10. We need flowers to bring the bees.
11. Rotate crops season to season, and within
    a season use crop succession to keep the
    garden producing.
12. Grow something new: You may not know
    how much you like kohlrabi.

CHAPTER SIX

Personal Best

MY SISTER, SHARI, IS INCREDIBLY TIDY. Summer holidays together are spent on the coast of Maine with our families in a cottage we rent each year. We have a great system in place that works well for both of us. I shop the farmers markets in Portland and cook whatever is in season, making a full, creative mess of the kitchen as I go, and she happily cleans up behind me. I say "happily" because the last thing she wants to do is cook and the last thing I want to do is clean. We are both happy with the results of our efforts: big family meals enjoyed by all, lots of laughter and music in the kitchen, a total engagement with the produce of the season, and a clean kitchen that awaits the preparation of the next meal.

Shari and I have joked about it over the years, but the truth is that too much order makes me uncomfortable. I like a bit of disorder, especially in the gardens. Perfect gardens, laid out in perfect rows, with equal amounts of this and that make no sense to me. I want garden magic—Bachelor Buttons popping up in unexpected places between the broccoli plants, scabiosas spilling up and over and through the herb patch. I love disorderly order, and guess what? It's good for your garden! Diversity is what our soil needs. Not the monoculture of the same plants planted all together from one season to the next, but instead a rich tapestry of plants from various families interplanted and moved about from season to season. That's how nature works in the wild: Any

piece of ground that is disturbed by fire or the plow will come roaring back with a vast array of plants that situate themselves in a new arrangement. That's a good way to think about your garden, too. Assume that these plants want to find their own arrangement and that it is happening through you. You are helping them distribute themselves like they would in a wild setting.

This is my aesthetic, and remember it is just that: my own. These are my own preferences, and just as I have mine, each gardener finds their own. As long as the plants are given enough room to grow and are planted in their proper season, the garden can be anything we want it to be.

Above Left
The disorderly order of a
beautifully planted garden

Above Right
Dahlias in bloom at Chase
Farm in Maine

Planting High and Low

As we discussed in the last chapter, seed packets generally tell us how far apart the vegetables or flowers need to grow. For example, broccoli should be planted at least 12 inches (30.5 cm) apart in a row and with rows at least 24 inches (61 cm) apart. These guidelines are a good place to start; over time you may find ways of grouping plantings closer together. Something I like to do is plant high and low. What I mean by this is if I am growing broccoli, which is tall, I can plant something low-growing such as nasturtium flowers or lettuce underneath. This makes the most of the growing space we have plus adds considerable beauty to the garden.

Planting in this manner also helps keep moisture in the soil by not allowing the sun to hit the soil directly. When the sun bakes the dirt, it dries out. The lettuce or nasturtium functions almost (but not quite) like mulch. The cabbage patch looks beautiful with dill planted in between the cabbage heads, and the dill also helps fend off pests. Aesthetically, it gives that spot in the garden an airy beauty with delicate leaves of fragrant dill coming up between the cabbage heads. Letting the dill go to flower adds even more magnificence to the garden. Try interplanting herbs and vegetables and find the combinations that appeal most to your sense of beauty.

For instance, I like planting borage flowers around the snap pea trellis. As the peas come into harvest, the borage blooms, with blue flowers opening up next to plump green peas on the trellis—a beautiful combination. Planting purple mizuna beneath and around the broccoli plants is also very pleasing to the eye, and they work well together in the garden and on the plate, too: mizuna dressed in an olive oil–lemon dressing with roasted broccoli on top!

Opposite
Beauty and flavor at every height: Climbing beans tower above favas and African basil, and low-growing strawberries spread across the surface of the soil. This arrangement makes excellent use of the growing space and protects some tender plants from harsh sun.

Below Left
Curled parsley forms a low, dense layer in the herb garden.

Below Right
Edible borage flowers. Borage grows up to three feet tall and is a great companion plant for tomatoes and peas.

Going to Seed

I am always excited for the new season. It doesn't matter which one is ending and which is on the horizon—the garden helps us to better understand and welcome endings and appreciate new beginnings. The warm season brings juicy tomatoes, which I have waited months for, but there is always that moment toward the end of summer when I have eaten more tomatoes than I believed possible, and thoughts of the arugula, carrots, and beet greens that come in the cooler months begin dancing through my head.

At the end of their growing cycle, these leafy greens, carrots, broccoli, and more bolt, growing up toward the sky and flowering. Their flowers produce the seeds for the next year's garden. Sometimes I just let them bolt. There is a wild and unique beauty in seeing these plants go to seed. I appreciate both the purpose and the reckless abandon they bring to the landscape.

It's an aesthetic that not everyone appreciates. In the school gardens where I teach, an important part of our curriculum is allowing plants to go to seed and harvesting those seeds for the following year. I once overheard a student's visiting family member complaining that there were plants in the garden going to seed and that someone should really pull those out. We each have our own interpretation of beauty. Nature has guided my aesthetic and I have found that when I am open to all the paths that plants take on their journey, even the unexpected ones, my own view of the world opens in unimaginable ways.

Opposite Left
Sage is especially beautiful when it flowers.

Opposite Right
Broccoli plants at the end of the season begin to bolt before flowering and going to seed.

Above
There is a wild and unique beauty in seeing plants go to seed. I appreciate both the purpose and the reckless abandon they bring to the landscape.

Maintaining the Garden

Caring for the garden regularly is essential for a healthy and bountiful garden. I like to start my day in the garden with my morning coffee. The first thing I do is walk through the garden to see what needs attention, what is ready to harvest, what should be pulled, and where there is room to do some new seeding.

Many people wonder how to tell when something is ready to harvest. For vegetables such as broccoli and cauliflower, the heads are ready to harvest when they are still dense, but may or may not be the size of what you are used to buying in the store. The important thing is to harvest the heads before they begin to open. Though still edible and delicious once they've opened, they are at their prime when the heads are still tight. Vegetables such as peas, cucumbers, and green beans will appear similar to what you normally purchase—they will just taste so much better! Tomatoes are ready when they are juicy and red (or yellow, orange, etc., depending on

the variety). Swiss chard and kale plants should be harvested from the outside in, leaving at least three or four leaves in the center so the plant knows to keep growing. The same is true for all leafy greens, including spinach, lettuce, and arugula. Root vegetables such as carrots and beets need to be checked by putting a finger into the soil at the base of the plant and touching the vegetable itself to see if it feels mature. As root vegetables reach maturity, their green tops will have grown tall, indicating the vegetable just below the surface is ready or nearly ready to pull from the soil.

After harvesting, address any issues such as aphids or other pests (more on that in Chapter Seven), remove dead leaves, and put in stakes or tomato cages for any plants that need support. Help climbing vines find the trellis they need to get off the ground. Feed your garden soil every two weeks with liquid seaweed to give plants the nutrient boost they need.

Opposite
I find tremendous satisfaction in working methodically through the garden, harvesting what's ready, trimming away dead leaves and vines, weeding, amending, and watering. The more attention you give the garden, the better you both do.

Above
Summer squash varieties include Black Beauty, Golden Zucchini, and Dario, and are best picked before they get too big.

A GARDEN CAN BE ANYWHERE

An Edible Landscape

The vegetable beds aren't the only places we can grow food. Look to the surrounding landscape for areas to plant favorite fruit trees and fruiting vines. Depending on where you live, you might try growing grapes on and over a pergola or raspberries, blackberries, and boysenberries on a fence. My husband grows a single boysenberry vine on the corner post of a porch that yields enough for about five pies every spring. Pomegranate, fig, and persimmon trees don't demand as much water as many other fruit trees and do well in more arid regions. Cherry, plum, nectarine, and peach trees bring spectacular flowers in the spring, followed by juicy, warm fruit in the summer months. Where possible, growing a few Eureka lemon, Meyer lemon, orange, tangerine, lime, and other citrus trees is a real treat, and they prove to be so useful when you can just dash out of the kitchen and grab a couple while cooking.

Left
Stone fruit trees make beautiful
flowers in the spring.

Page 196
Peaches ripening on the tree. Find
the varieties that are best for your
growing zone.

Page 197
Apple trees are a delicious and
beautiful addition to the landscape.

A GARDEN CAN BE ANYWHERE

Above
Every gardener finds the plants that give them the most pleasure, whether it is from the food they provide, the beauty they bring to the garden as they grow, or their scent.

Playing Favorites

Every gardener finds the plants that give them the most pleasure, whether it is from the food they provide, the beauty they bring to the garden as they grow, or their scent. My hope for every garden is that it provides my client with pleasures for all the senses—the softness of lamb's ear leaves on the skin; the scent released by herbs as they are clipped from the plant; the beauty of a single poppy in spring; the taste of freshly shucked peas; the bees making their exquisite buzzing roar as they work their magic.

Over the years, I have found my own favorites, just as you will discover yours. The joy of discovery happens every day in the garden. I practically run to the garden each morning to find out what has happened since the day before. The pleasures are endless.

AFRICAN BASIL

The first thing I plant when I begin a new garden is African basil. African basil is the heart of my gardens. More than any other flowering plant, its deeply fragrant purple flowers bring the bees. I see and hear hundreds of bees on any given African basil plant as I am working in the gardens. That is a glorious reassurance, the sight and sound of health, the true sign that the garden is working as it should. Without bees and other pollinators such as butterflies and even bats, our gardens and farms can't produce food. The bees carry life for us all as they float from flower to flower, pollinating the garden as they go. There are all kinds of estimates out there about how much bees contribute to our food supply—how they account for every third bite of food we take, for instance—but I don't think many of them are terribly accurate. Here's what is true: If it weren't for bees, we wouldn't have enough food to eat, and they are in trouble.

Accepting bees is an important step for all of us. Too many of us have learned to be frightened of bees and their stings, and the first thing we do when we see a beehive is call an exterminator to get rid of it. I teach both clients and kids in the school gardens that bees are so busy doing their hard work of gathering nectar and pollen that they are really not interested in us at all. Bees are in serious trouble right now because modern pesticides and habitat loss are causing their populations to crash, and we need to protect them in any way we can. If you think about the impossibility of hand-pollinating all the plants on Earth, you'll feel more strongly than ever about growing organic. We need to support these little miracles!

My client Penny had a deep dislike for bees. I planted African basil in her garden to encourage the bees to come and pollinate it. I explained to her how much we need bees. She tolerated them for the first couple of seasons and then she came to me and said that we needed to remove the African basil—the bees made her nervous. Until this point, her vegetable garden had flourished, providing Penny and her family with their favorite foods, including harvest baskets full of summer squash. I tried to convince her that the African basil should stay, but she wanted it removed and felt as though she had a healthy garden, so what could go wrong? As she requested, I removed the African basil and you can probably guess the result: The next season's planting of zucchini and other squash failed to thrive. There were no bees to pollinate their tender flowers. The squash either didn't form or yellowed and died on the vine.

Penny came to me, very concerned, and wanted to know what was wrong with her garden and what was wrong with the squash. I explained that in removing the African basil, we took away the bees' favorite flower and they were no longer pollinating the plants. Penny understood immediately why that African basil had been so vital to her garden. She asked to replant some that very same day and we got them back in the garden and got lucky: The bees returned and the next season, and every season since, her garden has produced more food than she and her family can even consume!

Our role as gardeners is to help nature along and then stand back and let the natural world work as it is meant to. In encouraging nature to do as it should, bees and all, we are also making a healthier world for ourselves and our planet.

Other Favorites

Here are some other vegetables and flowers that I love to plant in my gardens:

FAVA BEANS

They grow tall and wild, with exquisite flowers that produce the bean pods. They are packed with protein and can be used to make delicious spreads. My favorite recipe is Suzanne Goin's fava bean puree with feta, olives, and fresh garden herbs.

PURPLE SPROUTING BROCCOLI

Luscious, sweet, purple-hued, multi-sprouting broccoli. Good for overwintering.

POPPIES

Exotic ones. My favorites include Black Swan, Hungarian Bread Seed, Lauren's Grape, and Florist Pepperbox.

BORAGE

The entire plant is edible, and the flowers, in both white and blue varieties, are so pretty in salads. Plant borage near tomatoes as a companion plant. The flowers bring bees to the garden as well.

SCARLET RUNNER BEANS

Beautiful on a trellis with bright red flowers and incredible beans. Shell them or roast them whole to enjoy.

FENNEL

Prized by chefs, fennel comes in both bronze and green varieties. It is very sweet when roasted. Allow some to go to seed to use the flowers and seeds as well.

PURPLE CAULIFLOWER

Seeing the bright purple head of this variety of cauliflower come into harvest is one of the joys of gardening for me. It adds a huge burst of color to the garden and the plate.

SWEET PEA FLOWERS

These flowers smell like heaven, but don't eat them! They are not edible, but they are beautiful both in the garden or cut and put into vases around the house.

LISTADA DE GANDIA EGGPLANT

This is a gorgeous variety of Italian eggplant. Lavender and white stripes, very sweet.

BLACKBERRIES

There is nothing like a handful of warm berries just picked on a summer day. I love to pluck them off the vine and eat them in the garden or use them in a crostata.

ANISE HYSSOP

Bees and butterflies are both attracted to the edible purple flowers of anise hyssop. A widely used herbal remedy, fragrant and beautiful!

Fava beans

Purple sprouting broccoli

Fennel

Cauliflower

MIZUNA

A gentle spicy green. I like using both the green and purple varieties in fresh garden salads.

ARUGULA

Otherwise known as rocket, this is easy to grow and the spicy green leaves make for wonderful salads. It's delicious in pasta, too!

RAINBOW CHARD

Resilient and a good producer, I like to use rainbow chard in stir-fries with garlic, olive oil, and salt.

RED RUSSIAN KALE

A wonderful variety of kale that's versatile in the kitchen. Use for salads or sautés.

ROMANESCO

Breathtaking when coming into harvest with its spiraling heads, romanesco requires patience, but the rewards are great. I love roasting these and tossing with pine nuts, currants, and parsley.

SPIGARELLO

The sweet, tender, dark green leaves of broccoli spigarello are native to Italy. Delicious sautéed. One of my favorites.

GREEN ZEBRA TOMATOES

A really wonderful, sweet variety. I like slicing them and serving them simply dressed with good olive oil, salt, and basil, plus some crusty bread.

BROCCOLI

So many varieties to choose from! Try Belstar, Marathon, or Arcadia for large, dense heads and De Cicco for looser heads and long-producing side shoots.

MESCLUN

Easy to grow and wonderful in the kitchen for slightly spicy salads.

ARMENIAN CUCUMBERS

Large, light green cucumbers. Mild in taste and fun to grow.

LEMON CUCUMBERS

Round yellow cucumbers that have a bright flavor. One of my family's favorite varieties.

SPECKLED ROMAN TOMATOES

I like making long-cooked tomato sauces with this beautiful variety.

PINEAPPLE TOMATOES

Large, sweet, yellow tomatoes with pink striping inside.

INDIGO ROSE TOMATO

Dark purple tomatoes with red flesh. Dramatic addition to the summer garden.

CHIVES

I grow both onion and garlic varieties and use them in dressings, as garnishes, and for their flowers. Easy to grow and can be harvested in large quantities by cutting across the bottom of the plant. It will grow right back!

RED CABBAGE

This purple-headed variety of cabbage is a favorite in our house. I like using it to make a cabbage slaw for tacos.

CILANTRO

Use the leaves, then the flowers, and finally the fresh coriander seeds themselves.

Hyssop in bloom

Arugula

Striped Roman tomatoes

Red cabbage

Opposite
White borage flowers are edible and
make for a gorgeous presentation.

Above
Nigella flowers are among my
favorites.

Find Your Own Favorites

Consider this a place to begin. You will find your
own favorites, the plantings that bring you the
most pleasure. One of our joys, as gardeners, is to
look through the seed catalogs from the great seed
houses—Uprising Seed Co., High Mowing, Adaptive
Seeds, Hudson Valley Seed Co., Seed Savers—
fueling our imaginations with possibility and
wonder. A garden is very much rooted in the present
with an eye to the future and the hope that work
done today brings the bounty to come.

Garden Notes
1. Order vs. disorder: Everyone brings their
   personal tastes and styles to gardening.
2. Plant high and low to save space.
3. Letting plants go to seed brings
   beautiful flowers.
4. Maintain the garden by harvesting, weeding,
   pruning, and feeding with liquid seaweed.
5. Plant an edible landscape all around
   the property.
6. African basil is good for bees—and the heart of
   all my gardens.
7. Some of my other favorite vegetables, flowers,
   and herbs—see pages 200–201.

CHAPTER SEVEN

Gardening with Wildlife

WHEN WE CREATE A GARDEN, we are engaging with the natural world on a very intimate level. We are giving ourselves a front-row seat to nature's processes. For many of us, this is the first time in years, or ever, that we have been this close. In committing to the land in this way, we are able to see plants sprout from the soil after rains, food produced, new seeds created, and the whole food chain come to life before our eyes. A truth becomes evident as we watch the garden and all that surrounds it: *Everything wants to live.*

The plants struggle for water and sun and nutrients. We tend those plants because we can hardly wait to eat them. But insects and neighborhood animals also flock to gardens, looking for their own nourishment. The plants that feed us also look very appetizing to a vast array of other living creatures. We welcome the bee and butterfly, which pollinate our garden as they come through to sip a little nectar and gather pollen, but what about the deer, rabbits, mice, gophers, birds, and the like? Most of the time we are working to keep them out. How can we do so in a way that is in balance with nature?

Every garden will have a few visitors here and there, and that is generally not a problem. But there are times when a flock of starlings will devour your just-planted seeds or an ambitious deer will gnaw your vegetables right down to the dirt, and then— unless it is your goal to feed the wildlife, which is a noble thing to do but probably unnecessary—we have to protect the garden in order to have anything left to eat. Most of us want to eat from our gardens, so we need to discourage hungry critters from feasting on them while honoring the natural world around us.

First Do No Harm

In my gardens, I practice coexistence. That means we live with the creatures in the neighborhood, from bees to coyotes—and with other humans, too. I know that many people have grown up with farms in their families, and that farmers of another generation would kill a troublesome woodchuck or deer, but it's simply not necessary, and oftentimes it leads to some terrible, if unintended, consequences.

For instance, I am adamant about not using rodent poison as a way to keep rats or gophers out of the garden. Don't do it, and ask your neighbors not to do it, either! These poisons might eliminate a problem, but they create a bigger one: They work their way through our food chain, creating suffering and environmental harm as they go. Poisoned rodents end up killing hawks, owls, eagles, coyotes, dogs, cats, mountain lions, and more—the very predators that keep down the rodent population. A typical barn owl, for instance, lives for four years and eats about six mouse-size critters every night. That is thousands of rodents. But one poisoned rat can be the end of that owl. Without predators of all kinds, we cannot have a healthy ecosystem, so we need to find nontoxic ways to deal with our garden visitors and also to encourage natural controls. Rather than setting out poison, get together with your neighbors and put up a couple of owl nesting boxes. Invite them to the neighborhood!

Opposite
Bloomsdale spinach is an excellent producer and one of my favorite varieties, but snails and slugs also love to eat it.

Above
A garden house creates a protected outdoor space where some of the critters in the neighborhood just can't get in.

Tricks of the Trade

There are a bunch of humane solutions that will help keep critters out of the garden, and I encourage you to try them all to find out what works. These little tricks put you in communication with the wildlife: The two of you are trying to work out a problem together.

Raccoons and opossums are good creatures to have around, as they eat rodents and insects and any spilled food or mess that attracts pests; however, once in a while they will eat garden plants. I have found that placing a couple of bowls of water around the garden sometimes keeps them satisfied. The water doesn't work in every garden, but it might be enough to keep these curious animals occupied and away from the plants.

Critters are often averse to strong spices. Cotton balls soaked in mint oil are a deterrent—place them in and around the garden. Even better is to put out the mint balls and also sprinkle cayenne pepper around the edges of the garden bed and in between vegetables. Some people find that using crushed-up garlic in conjunction with chili powder works, too. The strong minty scent and the spicy tang of the pepper drive off many kinds of animal visitors. You will have to reapply them frequently, especially after rains and watering of the garden.

Netting

Using bird netting to cover tender baby seedlings helps keep not just birds but all animals away until the plants are larger and more mature, at which point they are less desirable to wildlife and more able to survive the loss of a few leaves. Lots of birds and other animals prefer the tiny seedlings and will pull them up or nip them off, and one good response is to place a trellis at the center of a garden bed as a support and drape the bird netting from the top of the trellis and down and around the entire garden bed, securing the bottom of the netting with rocks or other weighted objects. You'll have to fold back the netting when you work in the garden, but this is an incredibly effective and low cost method to protect crops, as the netting is inexpensive. Netting can also easily be wrapped over just-planted pots or set up like a tent over a newly planted patch of ground.

Opposite Top Left and Below
Using bird netting to cover the vegetable garden helps keep not just birds but all animals away.

Opposite Top Right
A harvest of Bloomsdale spinach and mizuna mustard greens

Gopher Wire

Gophers eat your crops from underneath, sometimes pulling whole plants into the ground like in a cartoon—*fwoop!* To stop them, place gopher wire on the bottom of all garden beds. This is the single most effective way to discourage gophers from coming to the garden. If they can't get to those tender plants through their subterranean tunnels, they go elsewhere. If you are planting directly into the ground, place a layer of gopher wire 1 foot (30.5 cm) below the surface: Roots will grow through it, but the plant will be protected.

Be sure to bring the gopher wire up to just beneath the surface of the soil at the edges of the garden plot. I also plant all fruit trees and fruiting shrubs, such as blueberries, in gopher wire.

Sonic spikes are sometimes effective in deterring moles or gophers. They are available online or in any garden shop. I have seen them successfully drive away pests, but I have also seen determined beasts dig holes right next to them, almost in defiance. I guess it depends on the sonic sensitivity of your pests.

Above Left
Hog wire fencing is a useful and beautiful option for enclosing garden beds.

Above Right
Drape netting over a free-standing trellis to keep it off the plants.

Fencing

When growing in an area frequented by roaming deer, a good sturdy fence is just about the only thing that's going to keep them out of your garden. A typical white-tailed or mule deer usually has plenty of the browse that it needs to stay alive out in the local wild, but they definitely prefer your veggies! They can smell that delicious vegetable garden from far away, and it beckons to them from the woods and hillsides where they live. When planning a new garden, if I know there are deer present, I build a fence into the garden plan right from the start.

There are many ways to fence, including wood, chain-link, or wire strand, or a garden house. The fencing you choose will be both a practical and an aesthetic decision: A chain-link fence, for instance, may be effective, but sometimes not as nice to look

at as a wood fence that can be repainted regularly or left to weather to a rustic patina. Deer are incredible jumpers and can easily clear an 8-foot (2.4-m) fence when they are really motivated. However, building a fence that high is not always possible and sometimes not allowed by local ordinances. A fence that tall may also be totally out of place for the look and feel of your home or garden space. Building a fence at least 6 feet (1.8 m) tall will help deter deer activity in the garden. Make sure your fence is secured at the bottom; deer regularly squeeze under fences that they can't get over. They are resourceful!

I love to put in a wood fence when I can, but a couple of my other favorites are chain-link planted with passion fruit vines or berry vines—which love to climb and change the whole aesthetic—and hog wire, with its pleasing square pattern.

Above
Jasmine climbing the garden fence.

A Garden House Offers Beauty and Protection

With deer wandering so many of the neighborhoods where I garden, I build a lot of garden houses. This is a beautiful solution to curious critters and transforms the garden into another living space.

A garden house is a completely enclosed structure that houses the vegetable garden. Think of a greenhouse, but with screens instead of glass. The screens have openings that allow the bees and butterflies in but keep out mice and anything bigger. I first saw a garden house at the home of my friend Jeff Martin. His was a simple and beautiful rectangular structure built by his father, architect Richard Martin. Since then, I've seen and built many variations of the garden house, each one customized for its particular location and use by the owners.

Jeff's home in LA's Laurel Canyon neighborhood is frequented by many deer, rabbits, and other canyon creatures. It was truly impossible for him to grow food without a structure that could completely enclose the garden, because those creatures were desperate to get at it. The walls and ceiling of a typical garden house are all made of screens, letting the light and elements in, yet keeping the wildlife out. The structure itself has a wood frame, which can be stained to tie in to the natural surroundings—think deep pine greens, bark browns, or a more dramatic statement that connects to architectural details of the home.

I build garden houses for clients all the time and there's no reason you can't build one yourself. They're not complicated. In fact, I'm including in this book an illustration showing one standard version of the house I build to help you build your own. This version works well in places with moderate climates such as California, Texas, and Florida, but it can also be modified to suit your climate. If you live somewhere like New York or Massachusetts, for example, consider building a version with a peaked or slanted roof made of glass or Plexiglas, with glass or Plexi storm-door attachments to hang on the sides that make it useful as a hothouse in the winter. Then you can remove the sides to let the garden breathe all summer.

This house also doesn't need to be freestanding, but could be built off the sunny side of a barn or garage.

When setting out to build a garden house, make sure it is in the area that receives the most hours of sun per day. If it's shaded, the plants are going to struggle. Then determine what size you need: If you are building raised beds in the garden house, how many are you putting in, how big are they, and how are you arranging them? Also, are you leaving any space for a little table and chairs? Some forethought can turn your garden house into a beautiful living and working space for your family.

Opposite
A garden house is a completely enclosed structure that houses the vegetable garden. Think of it as a greenhouse, but with screens instead of glass.

First of all, make sure to leave at least 3 feet (91 cm) between the door of the garden house and the start of the vegetable beds, so you have some space to work. Beds should have 2 feet (61 cm) between them. To save space, they can be placed against the walls of the garden house, and then the screens act like a trellis for vegetables such as peas, cucumbers, and beans to climb. I build the beds 18 inches (46 cm) high to make sure the roots of the plants have ample room to grow. The 22-foot (6.7-m) wide by 18-foot (5.5-m) long garden house in our illustration, for instance, has room for four beds that are each 15 feet (4.6 m) long and 3 feet (.9 m) wide. You can grow a lot of food in that amount of space.

The roof of the garden house should be at least 8 feet (2.4 m) high to accommodate the indeterminate height of tomatoes and runner beans. I build most garden houses at a height of 9 feet (2.7 m), as these tall plants often climb through the roof of the garden house and across the top! Be sure to get a sense of how the height of the garden house will work in your own landscape. Many times, a garden house feels less intrusive at 8 feet (2.4 m) tall and coping with wild climbing plants is still manageable.

When the garden house is completed, have a look at the screens. If they seem to really stand out in the yard, you can take the same paint or stain that you used on the framing and use it on the screens. This helps them blend in to the background.

Don't forget the flowers! Be sure to include flowers and African basil to bring bees into the garden so that the plants get lots of attention from these vital pollinators. Remember that this garden house is not sealed off from the outside; it's meant to fully communicate with all the natural processes outdoors while simply preventing invasion by curious nibblers.

Opposite
Plans for a 22 feet x 18 feet x 9 feet (6.7 m x 5.5 m x 2.7 m) garden house. These dimensions can be easily modified to suit your space. The $1/2$-inch (1.25-cm) steel wire mesh allows bees to get into the house but keeps out deer and other creatures.

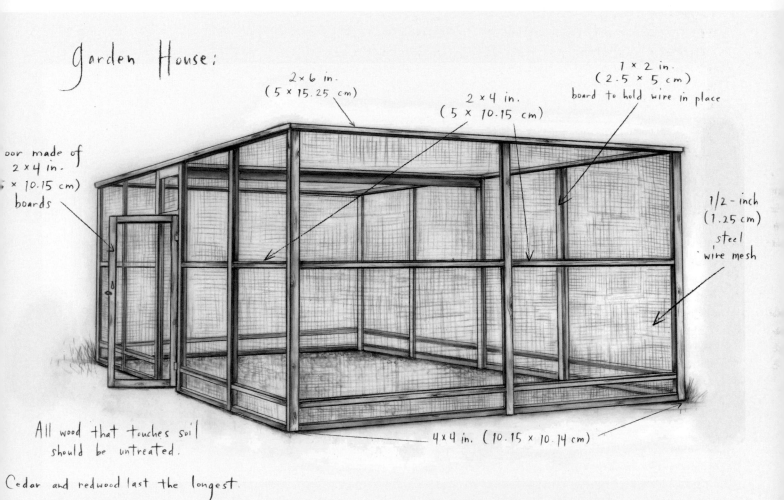

Garden House:

2 × 6 in.
(5 × 15.25 cm)

2 × 4 in.
(5 × 10.15 cm)

1 × 2 in.
(2.5 × 5 cm)
board to hold wire in place

oor made of
2 × 4 in.
× 10.15 cm)
boards

1/2 - inch
(1.25 cm)
steel
wire mesh

All wood that touches soil
should be untreated.

Cedar and redwood last the longest.

4 × 4 in. (10.15 × 10.14 cm)

Illustration: Paige Imatani

Even if we are successful at keeping the larger critters away, it is a normal part of the growing process that from time to time insects, snails, and other pests will make their way into the garden. When this happens, our gardens are trying to tell us something—maybe there is too much water or too little; perhaps the plants are stressed from unexpected weather or from crowding. This is a good time to fine-tune our approach to the garden while addressing the creatures at hand.

The treatments I use are designed to discourage bugs and keep them away, but sometimes, just like pulling a weed, those creatures are going to die. I don't take that lightly, and I try to let nature do that work as much as possible so that some other creature, such as a bird, will benefit.

For this and other reasons we've already discussed, it is essential that we stay far away from chemical pesticides or anything that is not organic. Even when using organic pesticides, be careful to apply them only at daybreak or in the early evening. Some organic pesticides are still harmful to bees and we want to take care to use them when bees are not visiting the garden.

Here are some pest treatments I use as needed, and which give me good results:

Neem spray. Neem is an oil pressed from the seeds of the neem tree, an evergreen in India. Like some other pine derivatives, bugs avoid it. I use neem for aphids, spider mites, and tent worms. Whatever spray or preparation you use, be sure to check that the only active ingredient in it is neem, as some have additional active ingredients that are still organic but are harmful to bees.

Beer. If you have a slug or snail problem, put a couple of bowls of beer in the garden. The mollusks absolutely love beer and will leave your plants alone.

Sluggo. This is iron phosphate, which is an organic nutrient for the soil and safe around pets and people. I use this for dealing with out-of-control snail problems when repeated uses of beer in small bowls prove futile.

Spinosad. This is isolated from a kind of bacteria and is usually pretty effective. I use spinosad when the bagrada bugs show up in the hot weather. I also use spinosad for caterpillars, beetles, and leaf miners. Spinosad is toxic to bees, so apply only in the evening and stay away from the flowering parts of the plants that bees are attracted to.

When you're working in the garden and find pests that are large enough to handle one at a time, such as tomato hornworms and other caterpillars, try picking them off and carrying them away from the garden to a place where birds will easily find them and enjoy a tasty meal. I do this when I'm digging in the garden and finding way too many grubs, as well. Some robust birds such as blue jays aren't shy; they'll come right over and grab them. The birds will thank you and maybe keep away from your newly planted seeds!

Good bugs. Just as we need to address the pests that visit our gardens, it is also important to encourage beneficial insects and bugs to make a home among our vegetable plants. Order some ladybugs and set them out in the garden as the sun sets and the air is cool. The heat of day is too hard on them and they will most likely fly away. Ladybugs love to eat the aphids that are plaguing your kale, broccoli, and cauliflower plants.

If praying mantises are not coming to your garden on their own, try ordering praying mantis eggs and place them in your garden beds. Praying mantises have big appetites and are happy to help out with the caterpillars, grasshoppers, beetles, and other bugs that are working their way through the garden.

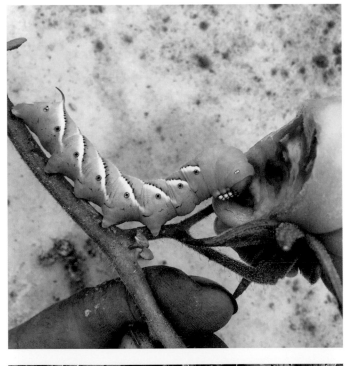

Above Left
Tomato hornworms strip tomato plants of their leaves and eat the tomatoes as they grow. Pull them off and put them far away from the garden.

Above Right
Snails are a common garden pest.

Below Left
Leaf damage from garden pests

Below Right
Slugs enjoy spinach, too.

Be Kind

Opposite
African basil

It can't be said enough. Causing harm to the living creatures around us causes harm to us all and to the Earth. Occasionally we kill a bug, but any measures to deal with animal intrusions in the garden need to be taken with compassion and kindness. Prevention is the best medicine.

Garden Notes

1. The strategy for dealing with wildlife is coexistence: Killing pests creates unintended consequences.
2. Never use poison!
3. Critters avoid mint and cayenne pepper.
4. Netting, gopher wire, and fences are effective barriers.
5. Garden houses are a beautiful solution.
6. Use organic solutions such as neem and spinosad for bugs.
7. Get good predators such as ladybugs and praying mantises.

A Visit to Chase Farm

with Meg Chase

The arrival of the fresh produce at Chase's Daily is one of those events around which lives are organized. Just before 11 A.M., the restaurant and market in Belfast, Maine's historic downtown is suddenly mobbed. Locals jam the handful of tables, ordering the gorgeous vegetarian menu items such as the curry fried rice or the goat cheese omelet, and line up to grab a coffee and a loaf of bread from the bakery. Meanwhile, the day's just-picked produce brought in from Chase Farm is set out in galvanized tubs and crates in the back of the old brick building. Folks sit on benches like bears on the riverbank awaiting the salmon run. And then the signal—open!—and they rush in, filling bags and baskets in a friendly frenzy. The hunter-gatherer spirit is alive and well!

For years, I have made the pilgrimage to Chase's Daily for the fresh food and for the palpable sense of mission there. The farm-restaurant-market operation was co-founded by Penny and Addison Chase, their daughters Meg and Phoebe, and Meg's partner, Freddy LaFage; on the company website, Meg writes of their commitment to slow growth, sustainability, and accessibility to food and to "cussed pursuit of quality," evident in every outrageous tomato and amaranth in their market. I have always admired the Chases' honesty, as they are not an all-organic farm but are still so committed to soil health and beautiful food at affordable prices. Even though Belfast is less a blue-collar town than it once was, they don't assume people can afford to pay top dollar. But I never grasped the scale of their commitment until I saw Chase Farm, a few miles away in Freedom, Maine.

Opposite
Meg Chase of Chase Farm

Above
Flower fields at Chase Farm

A GARDEN CAN BE ANYWHERE

On the August day when we arrived, the farm was an explosion of barely domesticated wildness, acre upon acre of hand-tended vegetables and a riot of flowers in variety after variety, row upon row of crops popping through a ground-warming cover of black plastic that wraps the raised beds. The spaces between rows were thick with cover crops of rye grass and berseem clover swarmed by burdock and other weeds—you could hardly tell one row from the next. Beautiful! A profusion of glorious life covered every square inch of soil.

No one showed us around on the day of our visit; no one had time. The crops are largely hand-tended and the scale is enormous. Penny and Meg greeted us and went back to picking; Addison and other family members and hired hands were scattered through the fields, hustling with armloads of beautiful cabbages and chard and dahlias. Phoebe and Freddy were already at the restaurant, where she is the baker and he cooks and runs the kitchen. When we got a chance later to talk more with Meg via email, she pulled no punches. As much as the Chases focus on soil health, they also worry about community access to food. "Fresh produce is for the rich," she wrote to us.

"I am comfortable with how we grow our products," Meg added. "Every choice we make is complicated and considered. Being organic gives you parameters to follow but doesn't ensure that your processes are sustainable. You can be a good conventional farmer and a bad organic one, and the opposite. I want to reach more people with lower prices. I am always on the lookout for systemic efficiencies to keep farming at our scale viable."

Above
"I think what people—potential employees and customers—want to know is, 'Are you a good farmer?' Yes, I am. We are."
—Meg Chase

Opposite
Wild carrot flowers

Talking with Meg revealed that a commitment to a living soil sometimes means using plastic instead of other kinds of mulch. I don't grow that way, but I also don't grow so many acres.

"Plastic mulch is a mainstay of our system," Meg wrote. "A petroleum product that provides weed control, prevents nutrient leaching, provides additional warming of the soil, and a conservative approach to irrigation. Also, the cover crops between the rows, which we purposely space farther apart than strictly necessary, ensure that nearly half of our arable ground is in cover crops each year. Bare, weed-free ground between row crops is soil that isn't being optimized. Living soil can only live if it has a plant growing in it or an organic mulch like straw covering it. The scale we wish to grow precludes the use of straw as mulch. Also, straw keeps the ground cool and harbors slugs and snails."

On the Chase Farm, they do use chemical fertilizers as well as a whole spectrum of organic and other sources for N, P, K, and other nutrients. Their approach to inputs changes, however, and not for the reasons you might imagine.

"We do use chemical fertilizer, but not in a vacuum of awareness concerning soil vitality," Meg wrote. "This year we are even considering switching to mainly organic sources for our nutrient inputs. Not necessarily because they are more conductive to achieving the quality of produce we seek, but in order to attract the farm help we need. The concept of 'organic inputs' is easier to get behind than 'chemical fertilizer.' Labor and the ability to attract and retain good workers is the looming limit of our ability to farm well and produce on the scale we have been achieving for the last fifteen years or so."

Above
Chase Farm is committed to slow growth, sustainability, and access to affordable food.

Opposite
Garlic drying on a rack

She added, "Sources of nitrogen include: liquid cow manure for our cover-cropped fields (not legal to use where food crops will be grown in the same year), soybean meal (for potatoes and other row crops that don't use plastic mulch, as it is a slow release source of nitrogen that is less likely to leach from the soil), fish meal (for the orchard which I manage organically, or really holistically, based on the books by Michael Phillips), cottonseed meal for the high bush blueberries, liquid fish and kelp for foliar feeding to adroitly address nitrogen deficiencies, and cover crops to enhance the microbial health in the soil to harness and convert atmospheric nitrogen. We use compost from Kinney Compost in our hoop houses and greenhouses and on perennial crops where the impact may justify the significant cost."

The Chase approach was fascinating, and the results incredible. This one farm stocked the restaurant and market in Belfast, day after day. They didn't serve meat, but they also weren't strictly vegan (they served eggs and cheese, for example) nor making special gluten-free or nightshade-free foods. "We're not purists," she said.

But they are New Englanders, through and through. There was a humility in their work that I love, that Meg said expressed itself as "pragmatism, compromise, thrift, work ethic, disdain for entitlement, diligence, quality." They make an ordinary business out of growing and cooking extraordinary food, and that has changed a whole town, and the way I look at farming. As she wrote to us, "I think what people—potential employees and customers—want to know is, are you a good farmer? Yes, I am. We are."

Above Left
Just-picked lettuces

Above Center
Fresh shallots

Above Right
Just in from the field, beets are washed and packed for transport to Chase's Daily.

Opposite
The morning's harvest is packed and headed to Chase's Daily in Belfast, Maine.

Page 230
The day's farm offerings at Chase's Daily

Page 231
Farm flowers are part of the reason people line up for Chase's opening each morning.

CHAPTER EIGHT

Community

Gardens Are Community

When I first moved to Los Angeles from New York City, I found it hard to connect to the new world around me. I was used to the energy and fast pace of my old city—the constant contact with people on the streets, on the subway, and in the crowded neighborhood coffeehouse. In Los Angeles there were people everywhere, but the connections I made felt very much on the surface of things. It wasn't until I found my way into the garden that my new home began to make sense.

When you plant a garden, a new community quickly organizes around it. The neighbor passing by your front-yard vegetable garden will call out and say how wonderful it smells as you are harvesting the rosemary, sage, and thyme or pulling mature onions from the soil. One of my favorite scents is the smell of onions as they let go of the earth that fed and nurtured them. The garden seems to demand meaningful connections with other creatures and ideas and people: Soon the farmers at the weekly farmers market who grew beautiful food and the folks at the local nurseries became trusted sources of garden wisdom and close friends. Clients spent time with me in their gardens and welcomed me into their homes, and many became cherished friends, too. Schools invited me to create gardening curriculums and teach kids what it means to grow your own food, and it is such a privilege to share this experience with so many families. Seeing the kids for years afterward is so life-affirming! I could never have imagined that by planting seeds in the soil a whole new world would be created. Now I can't imagine a life without gardens.

Opposite
Having friends to dinner out in the edible garden, with the smell of Meyer lemon blossoms, honeysuckle, and mint growing just next to the table, adds so much beauty and connection to a meal shared together.

That community grows like a garden grows, with a kind of invisible magic. This is why I am always so excited to plant a new garden, laying in the first seeds. For some time, the garden just looks like smoothed-over dirt with maybe a couple of seedlings sticking out. But then comes the invisible magic. I get such a thrill knowing that in a few months, those hidden seeds will create a beauty and bounty that changes everyone who is aware of it, from the family that is eating the vegetables to the passersby who smell a gorgeous flower.

We are all changed by the beauty of gardens. Gardens offer us hope and the possibility of what can be. It's a kind of guarantee that the basic processes of the earth still work fine: You put a seed in the ground and it grows food and new seeds. The world makes and remakes itself over and over, always new. If it's been a bad day, or even a bad year, come sit in the garden. Be part of the renewal. Dig in the soil. Feed it well with compost and alfalfa and it will feed you, in so many different ways.

This power of gardens keeps reasserting itself in my life. A few years back, I was going through a difficult time, a divorce and the rebuilding of a life with my two sons. I didn't have a real sense of how things would turn out. But being in the garden every day, caring for the plants and helping others grow nourishing food, took me from that place and carried me to another. The gardens were a living, breathing thing, and their energy and their needs and their sustenance brought me through. The flowers, fruit, and vegetables that came out of the soil were proof that I was on the right track, that some part of this was going to work fine. As the gardens grew, I grew. I was able to buy a house on my own for my kids and me to live in, my business grew, and I met the man who would become my husband and together we wrote this book. New possibilities kept opening up for me, assuring me that I was on the path I was meant to be on. Ultimately, the gardens led me to happiness.

Above
In school gardens, kids learn what it means to grow their own food.

Opposite
Farmers markets are a great source of connection for gardeners. This is Peter Schaner of Schaner Farms, one of the great California farmers and a generous teacher of how to grow good vegetables.

Above
Cactus paddles, or sopas, are great
grilled in tacos or salads.

Opposite
Onion flowers are a delicious addition
to soups and salads, and are also
beautiful in a vase.

Around our house, we've been reading a lot about
Aldo Leopold and his beautiful book, *A Sand County
Almanac*. It's more than a book of great animal
stories; it's the story of a garden. Leopold was one
of the first modern wildlife scientists to look not
simply at individual species but at how all the lives
in a neighborhood supported one another in what
he called the "biotic community." Leopold wrote *A
Sand County Almanac* from the experiences of his
family as they restored the native trees and grasses
on his tired-out corn farm along the Wisconsin
River. Their garden was a pine forest and a prairie,
and it took long years of hard work, but what strikes
me is that the five Leopold children took such joy
in the place. They loved being there and they loved
working in that sandy earth!

Leopold wrote in "The Land Ethic," an essay in the
book, that it is the whole community that matters
and deserves protection, and this community starts
with the land itself. Working a plot of soil puts us in
contact with the entire neighborhood: the plants,
bugs, soil chemistry, weather, animals, people—
everything. It's not an exaggeration to say that
gardening is a way to grow a family.

A Place for Living

More and more often, clients are asking me to build dining areas into garden plans so that they can entertain in these green spaces. Having friends to dinner out in the edible garden, with the smells of Meyer lemon blossoms, honeysuckle, and mint that are growing just next to the table, adds so much beauty and connection to a meal shared together. The food on your plate takes on added meaning and even tastes better when you see it growing in the vegetable beds all around the table!

Gardening is contagious. Once you've had your hands in the soil, you'll want to do it some more. It changes the way you see a piece of land, your food, the weather, grocery stores, everything. You have a new awareness of your food and respect for how it was grown. I have seen it happen over and over again: One family builds a vegetable garden and then their friend comes over and sees that garden and then they build a garden of their own. Soon, another friend sees the new garden and decides to build one, and on and on and on. Community gardens are fantastic resources, and they usually have waiting lists to get a garden plot to tend. The desire to grow one's own food is stronger than ever.

Remember the movie *Field of Dreams*? The line "If you build it, he will come" is pretty unforgettable. This idea proves true time and time again when it comes to gardens. We all want to create that space where hope, meaning, and happiness exist, and a connection to both the past and the future, and a garden can be this space. A garden brings us all together. Friends come for a meal or we bring them a basket of freshly harvested cucumbers, tomatoes, and beans. We talk about how delicious it is, how it was grown—we connect. Not only do we connect to each other; we connect back to the Earth. We are grounded by the knowledge that there is a process to life that is continuous and unwavering, no matter what else is swirling around us.

People want to spend time in a garden. They are attracted to it, even if they don't fully understand why. It is a place of refuge, contemplation, and mystery.

Opposite Left and Below Left
Gardens bring happiness.

Opposite Right
Passion flowers are a gorgeous table accent or, as created here by Louesa Roebuck, a boutonniere.

Below
A fistful of flowers changes an event or a room.

Page 244
Lilacs from the local farmers market

Page 245
A garden connects the house to the outdoors.

Music in the Garden

I am grateful for what the gardens teach me every day—year after year, every season, something new. I am also grateful for the unexpected people they've brought into my life.

I met Anne Litt, an amazing woman and DJ at KCRW in Los Angeles, because of gardens. She asked me to help her turn some unused land at her home in Hollywood into a place for growing food. We were digging up a hillside at her canyon home together, working for hours, just the two of us, doing a double dig so we could plant the soil with corn. It was grueling work, but we talked all the way through. This is how gardens foster friendships.

I was a songwriter and performer in another part of my life, and Anne and I bonded over our love of music. By the end of that first day, we'd come up with an idea to meld music and gardening into

something that would raise food and funds for those in need. The idea would become Music in the Garden, a series of concerts in both private homes and public spaces where admission would be a bag of food from your local farmers market or your own garden, or a monetary donation of any size that would go toward feeding the hungry. This made the events inclusive for anyone who wanted to participate—no massively expensive ticket cost to gain entry, just a desire to do good.

Below
Anne Litt and I planning our *Music in the Garden* concert series at the venue—a garden with a view of Los Angeles

The first concert was held in a private home and attended by around a hundred people, and the most recent was at LA's Natural History Museum and attended by thousands. The food people bring is donated to Project Angel Food and local food pantries, and the funds are donated to the Los Angeles Food Bank and also to a charity chosen by the musicians who perform. The success of these nights showed me how deep the connections are between people, gardens, giving, and community.

See for yourself. Take this book outside and find the spot for your garden. Put yourself into that space and see what you get back. With a little shovel work and a little attention, you're going to get a lot of delicious meals, and who knows what else? There is a community out there waiting to gather 'round. Put that seed in the ground and let the invisible magic happen.

Garden Notes

1. When you plant a garden, a new community forms around it.
2. A garden is the root of the biotic community.
3. Gardens are a place for living: planting, cooking, dining.
4. Invisible magic happens from the moment we plant the first seed.

Opposite
Gardens give us a new way of seeing.

Index

Acknowledgments

Eternal gratitude to Anjelica Jiminez, without whom none of this happens, and to our dear parents and families, especially my sister, Shari St. Amand.

Deepest appreciation to everyone who ever asked me to help them with a garden; and to my agent, Katherine Cowles; and Shawna Mullen and the crew at Abrams; and to designer Sean Adams; photographers Yoshihiro Makino and Brian Ferry; prop stylist and set designer Amy Elise Wilson; and illustrator Paige Imatani.

Heartfelt thanks to the colleagues, friends, and loved ones who have been there every step of the way, including:

Misael Valenzuela
Andrea Passarella
Suzanne Goin
David Lentz
Gloria Walther
Yuka Izutsu
Valerie Gordon
Stan Weightman Jr.
Brian Ferry
Shiva Rose
Lisa Rosenstein
Kim Feldman
Jessica Amisal
Sunset Nursery and the staff there, including
  Jim Mortimer, Dennis Kuga, Sally Melcher,
  and Rod Kitamura
Jeri Heiden
Ambre Dahan
Tori Horowitz
Shana Weiss
John Silva
Roberto Maiocchi
One Digital Farm
Heather Heron
Amy Dov
Sal Melendez
Benny Bohm
Lindsey Strasberg
Joe Dahan
Alexis Olyphant
Jo Strettell
Evan Funke
Lauren Hardman
Louesa Roebuck
Curtis Fletcher

Pamela Shamshiri
Matthew Brown
Peter Lee
Peter Schaner and Schaner Farms
Alex Weiser and Weiser Family Farms
Beth Schiller and Dandelion Spring Farm
Meg Chase and Chase Farm
  and Chase's Daily
James Birch and Flora Bella Farms
Molly Ford
Ruth Black
Todd Black
Katie Tarses
Anne Litt
Howard Franklin
Jo Abellera
Jenni Kayne
Richard Ehrlich
Mickey Hargitay
Jimmy Williams
Joel Shearer
Catherine McCord
Jamie Tarses
Lorena Barrientos
Agnes Baddoo
Ann Summa
Jeff Spurrier
Wendy Polish
Mark Polish
Victoria Morris
Zak Cook
Sheryl Sokoloff
Eve Gerber
Colleen Bennett
Lauren Soloff
Leanne Citrone
Samantha and Mario Caldato Jr.
Echo Park Craft Fair
Amy Dickerson

About the Authors

Lauri Kranz, founder of Edible Gardens LA, designs, builds, and sustains edible landscapes and vegetable gardens for chefs, restaurants, museums, schools, and private clients interested in growing their own food. For many years, she toured and recorded with her band, Snow & Voices. Lauri lives with her husband Dean and their family in Los Angeles' Laurel Canyon, where owls and coyotes sing their songs in the night.

Dean Kuipers writes about nature, art, and politics. He is the author of *Burning Rainbow Farm*, and his work has appeared in *Outside, Orion, Rolling Stone,* the *Los Angeles Times*, and many other publications. He and his wife, Lauri, take their three boys into the wild outdoors at every opportunity.

Yoshihiro Makino was born and raised in Tokyo, and he travels the world shooting architecture, landscapes, art, and portraits. His work has appeared in *Architectural Digest, Dwell, Wallpaper, WSJ. Magazine*, and many other publications. He has recently published landscape images from Peru and a book on Le Corbusier's Chandigarh. He lives in Los Angeles.

Visit Lauri and Edible Gardens LA at www.ediblegardensla.com.

Praise for *A Garden Can Be Anywhere*

"Lauri has helped us bring our garden to life! A vegetable garden is truly a spectacle to marvel at. A great display of nature's scenery, pure growth, and raw beauty and a human's display of endless dedication, tried patience, passionate commitment, and absolute love. What you put into your garden you will receive back plentifully."

—ROSIE HUNTINGTON-WHITELEY, MODEL, ACTOR, DESIGNER, AND JASON STATHAM, ACTOR, PRODUCER

"How very delicate and miraculous nature is . . . to not take for granted
as I've watched seeds to harvest.
this cycle of life running its course in front of me . . .
the taste of organic vegetables grown in my garden—kind of like
tasting for the first time . . .
a tomato . . . a cucumber
the blossom of a zucchini—
that hot peppers have white delicate flowers . . .
the bees, all of the creatures I never take a moment to notice . . .
Lauri has brought this awareness, gentle, powerful, magical beauty,
of this perfect eco system, perfect nature,
into my garden, into my life."

—NINA GARDUNO, FOUNDER AND DESIGNER OF FREECITY

Editor: Shawna Mullen
Designer: Sean Adams
Production Manager: Rebecca Westall

Library of Congress Control Number: 2018936228

ISBN: 978-1-4197-3319-2
eISBN: 978-1-68335-523-6

Printed and bound in China
10 9 8 7 6 5 4 3 2 1

Abrams books are available at special discounts when
purchased in quantity for premiums and promotions as
well as fundraising or educational use. Special editions
can also be created to specification. For details, contact
specialsales@abramsbooks.com or the address below.

Abrams® is a registered trademark of
Harry N. Abrams, Inc.

ABRAMS
The Art of Books

195 Broadway
New York, NY 10007
abramsbooks.com